The German State On A National And Socialist Foundation

New Approaches To The State, Finance And Economy.

Translated with a
Preface
by
Alexander Jacob

The German State On A
National And Socialist Foundation
New Approaches To The State,
Finance And Economy.

Translated with a
Preface
by
Alexander Jacob

Copyright © 2019 Sanctuary Press Ltd

All rights reserved. No part of this book may be reproduced in any form by any electronic or mechanical means including photocopying, recording, or information storage and retrieval without permission in writing from the publisher.

ISBN-13: 978-1-913176-22-8

Sanctuary Press Ltd
71-75 Shelton Street
Covent Garden
London
WC2H 9JQ

www.sanctuarypress.com
Email: info@sanctuarypress.com

Index

Preface by Alexander Jacob	5
Preface to Fifth Edition - Gottfried Feder	17
Foreword – Adolf Hitler	17
Introduction	19

I. The Foundations
- The Moral Foundations — 21
- The Economic Foundations — 26
- On The Boundaries Of The State And The Economy — 31
- The National Political Foundations — 37
- Insights And Goal-Setting — 45

II. The Programme
- The Origin Of The Programme — 51
- The National And Economic Programme of the National Socialist German Workers' Party — 53

III. The State Structure Of The National Socialist State
- The National Socialist Idea Of The German State — 59
- The Nationalist Idea — 61
- The Citizenship Right — 68
- The National Economy — 72
- National Financial Reform – Money And Credit in The National Socialist State — 84
- The National Financial Economy — 90
- The Versailles Dictate — 95
- The Loan Economy — 100
- The Reichsbank Corporation — 111
- Inflation — 113
- National Financial Reform — 118
- New Ways — 129
- The Social Construction And Economic Bank — 139
- The State Without Taxes — 148
- The Financial Political Liberation Of The State — 155

Preface

by Alexander Jacob

Gottfried Feder was born in 1883 in Würzburg and studied engineering at the Technical Universities in Munich, Berlin and Zurich. After the completion of his studies he set up a construction company of his own in 1908 under the aegis of Ackermann and Co. and undertook several projects in Bulgaria. From 1917 onwards he taught himself financial politics and economics and, in late 1918, not long after the proclamation of the Weimar Republic by Philipp Scheidemann in November of that year, Feder wrote a manifesto on usury[1] and sent it to the Kurt Eisner government, though he obtained no response. The Treaty of Versailles signed in June 1919 which determined Germany as solely responsible for the war and liable to reparations caused Feder to fear that Germany was now firmly in the hands of the international financiers. In September of that year, Feder established a militant league (Kampfbund) for the breaking of interest slavery and the nationalisation of the state bank. His anti-capitalism was bound also to racialism insofar as the international financiers were considered to be mostly Jews.

Feder's nationalist efforts drew him into a close alliance with the anti-Communist activist Anton Drexler (1884-1942) and Dietrich Eckart (1868-1923), the editor of the anti-Semitic journal Auf gut deutsch and later, of the National Socialist organ, Völkischer Beobachter. The three together formed, in January 1919, the Deutsche Arbeiter Partei (DAP).[2] Adolf Hitler joined the DAP in late September 1919 and soon emerged as the leader of the party, which he renamed the Nationalsozialistische Deutsche Arbeiterpartei (NSDAP). Hitler had, even before his joining the party, attended Feder's lectures on economic subjects and wrote later in his Mein Kampf (1925/6) of this occasion:

---

1   *Manifest zur Brechung des Zinsknechtschaft des Geldes*, Diessen vor München: Joseph C. Huber, 1919; cf. *Manifesto for Breaking of the Financial Slavery to Interest*, tr. Alexander Jacob, London, Black House Publishing, 2015

2   Another major early member was Karl Harrer (1890-1926), who joined the party in March of 1919. Harrer, like Drexler, was a member of the occultist Thule society in Munich, which was an off-shoot of the Germanen Order founded in 1912 by Theodor Fritsch. Eckart too was influenced by the doctrines of the Thule society.

Preface

For the first time in my life I heard a discussion which dealt with the principles of stock-exchange capital and capital which was used for loan activities ...The absolute separation of stock-exchange capital from the economic life of the nation would make it possible to oppose the process of internationalization in German business without at the same time attacking capital as such, for to do this would jeopardize the foundations of our national independence. I clearly saw what was developing in Germany and I realized then that the stiffest fight we would have to wage would not be against the enemy nations but against international capital.[3]

In the Foreword to the original 1923 edition of the current work, *Der deutsche Staat*, Hitler wrote that in this work the National Socialist movement had indeed acquired its "catechism".[4]

In 1920, Hitler, along with Feder and Drexler, composed the 25 point *'Programme of the NSDAP'*. This programme rejected the Treaty of Versailles and called for a reunification of German peoples along with an exclusion of aliens, especially Jews, from national life. In February 1920, Hitler held a rally in which he presented the programme to the German people. Later, in 1927, Feder published a comprehensive version of the programme entitled Das Programm der NSDAP and seine weltanschaulichen Grundlagen.[5] In 1923, Feder offered a further elaboration of his national economic views in the present work, *Der deutsche Staat auf nationaler und sozialer Grundlage*, which was re-issued in 1932 in the "Nationalsozialistische Bibliothek" series[6]

Feder took part in Hitler's failed Beer Hall Putsch against the Bavarian government in 1923 but was only fined 50 marks for unlawful assumption of authority since he had acted, for a day, as the new "finance minister". In 1924, he was elected a representative to the parliament. In parliament, he demanded the confiscation of Jewish property and the freezing of interest-rates. which were key elements of the anti-capitalist programme of the party. In 1926 Hitler entrusted Feder with the editorial direction of a series of books on National

---

3   Adolf Hitler, *Mein Kampf*, tr. James Murphy, London: Hurst and Blackett, 1939, pp.168,171.

4   See below p.17.

5   This work was translated by E.T.S. Dugdale as *The Programme Of The Nsdap And Its General Conceptions*, Munich, 1932.

6   I have for my translation used the 1932 edition, vol.35 of the "Nationalsozialistische Bibliothek" series.

The German State on a National and Socialist Foundation

Socialist ideology under the title "Nationalsozialistische Bibliothek" (National Socialist Library). In 1931, Feder was appointed chairman of the economic council of the NSDAP. But gradually, under pressure from big industrialists like Gustav Krupp, Fritz Thyssen and Emil Kirdorf, Hitler decided to distance himself from Feder's socialist ideas.[7] With Hitler's strategic alliance with big industrialists and capital, even foreign capital, for his intended war on Bolshevism, Feder lost most of his influence on the party since foreign banks especially would not have supported Feder's plans for a nationalised interest-free banking system. The loss of interest in Feder's economic policies among the party members is evidenced in Hans Reupke's book *Der Nationalsozialismus und die Wirtschaft* (!931), where the author stated that it was no longer necessary to deal with the "breaking of interest slavery" in "the extreme form in which it first emerged".[8]

Thus, when Hitler assumed power in 1933, Feder was not named Economics Minister but rather only State Secretary in the Economics Ministry. However, Feder published in 1933 a collection of his essays entitled *Kampf gegen die Hochfinanz* as well as a book on the Jews called *Die Juden*. In 1934, the influential banker Hjalmar Schact was made Economics Minister since his contacts with the big industrialists made him more useful to Hitler in his rearmament aims than Feder with his stark anti-capitalist doctrines. Feder's subordination to Hjalmar Schacht was indeed a concrete sign of his fall from grace. After the Knight of the Long Knives in 1934, when left-wing nationalists like Gregor Strasser were assassinated, Feder withdrew from the government. In 1936, he was given a new job as professor at the Technical University in Berlin which he maintained until his death in 1941.

Feder's *Deutsche Staat* is indeed one of the most important treatises on National Socialist economics.[9] However, it has a precedent in

---

7   For the part played by big industries in Hitler's rise to power see G. Hallgarten, "Adolf Hitler and German heavy industry 1931-1933", *Journal of Economic History*, 12 (1952).

8   H. Reupke, *Der Nationalsozialismus und die Wirtschaft*, Berlin, 1931, pp.29ff.

9   The closest to National Socialist economics is the Social Credit movement founded in Britain by C.H. Douglas (1879-1952), whose work *Economic Democracy* was published in 1920 (see F. Hutchison and B. Burkitt, *The Political Economy of Social Credit and Guild Socialism*, London: Routledge, 1997). Douglas influenced Oswald Mosley's British Union of Fascists in the thirties (see Kerry Bolton, "Breaking the bondage of interest, part 2", *Counter-Currents,* August 11, 2011, http://www.counter-currents.com).

the Austro-Hungarian Bohemian German, Rudolf Jung's work, *Der Nationale Sozialismus* (1919). Rudolf Jung (1882-1945) was a civil engineer from Jihlava (in the current Czech Republic and former Austro-Hungarian Empire) who joined the Bohemian Deutsche Arbeiter Partei (DAP) in 1909. The DAP was founded in 1903 in Aussig (now Ústí nad Labem in the Czech Republic) by Germans threatened by the increasing Jewish and Czech influence in the empire. It was renamed Deutsche Nationalsozialistische Arbeiter Partei (DNSAP) in 1918. Jung's work *Der Nationale Sozialismus: seine Grundlagen, sein Werdegang und seine Ziele* (1919) was intended as a German nationalist answer to Marx's *Das Kapital*.[10] The work is divided into two parts, the first dealing with 'The Foundations of National Socialism' and the second with 'The Development and Goals of National Socialism'. Jung's nationalism focusses on social and economic questions and, exactly like Feder, Jung stresses the difference between income derived from real work and that arising from interest.[11] His strong socialist and anti-Jewish viewpoint is evident throughout this work:

> All non-socialist parties are based in the main on "individualism", i.e. the demand for the greatest possible freedom and lack of constraint of the individual. Economically it is expressed in Manchester liberalism and, further, in Mammonism. The ruthless ruler who is tormented by no pang of conscience is the goal, the weaker man falls thereby under the wheels. Now, since the Jew is the most ruthless, he can fare best thereby. Thus all non-socialist anti-Jewish orientations unwillingly support the rise of Jewry to world-rulership.[12]

Further, democracy itself is the vehicle of Jewish international capitalism:

> If we were to sum up, we might say that the entire international democracy whose alleged ideals the major press and parties represent and on whose flag they swear, is nothing but the political

---

com/2011/08/breaking-the-bondage-of-interesta-right-answer-to-usury-part-2/

10 It was on his suggestion that Hitler changed the name of the German branch of the DAP in 1920 to Nationalsozialistische Deutsche Arbeiterpartei (NSDAP).

11 Feder's manifesto on interest-slavery was interestingly published in the same year as Jung's work on National Socialism.

12 Rudolf Jung, *Der Nationale Sozialismus*, Munich, 1922, p.187f.

crystallisation of the Jewish spirit and, in the final analysis, serves no other goal but the establishment of the world-rule of Jewry.[13]

Another writer who contributed to the exact identification of the Jewish constitution of international high finance was Heinrich Pudor (1865-1943), who also wrote under the pseudonym Heinrich Scham (the German translation of the Latin "pudor"). Pudor was a vegetarian and naturist who, from 1912, published several anti-Semitic pamphlets and books including an extensive series on the international connections between the various Jewish high financiers.[14] Feder refers sympathetically to Pudor in the present work.[15] However, Pudor's magazine *Swastika* was banned in 1933 by the National Socialists for its criticisms of the National Socialist leadership and the regime's surprising toleration of Jews. Further, five issues of the series on Jewish high finance were banned including no.13, *Neues über Br. Roosevelt und seine jüdischen und Kommunistischen Verbindungen*, and no.49, *Judendämmerung. "Juden unerwünscht". Keine jüdischen Rechtsanwälte mehr. Ende der Judenfinanz in Deutschland*, on account of what a state official, Raymund Schmidt, described as Pudor's "no longer opportune polemical methods which were indeed exploited by the English recently for the purpose of counter-propaganda.[16]

---

13 *Ibid.*, 53f.

14 The pamphlets that he self-published (in Leipzig) in this series, "Die internationalen verwandtschaftlichen Beziehungen der jüdischen Hochfinanz" ('The international kindred relationships of Jewish high finance'), between 1933 and 1940 present short historical accounts of the different branches of Jewry in various countries of Europe as well as in America. For instance, the first pamphlet is on *Das Haus Rothschild*, numbers two to four on *Ginsberg und Günsberg und Asher Ginzberg*, five to eight on *Jakob Schiff und die Warburgs und das New Yorker Bankhaus Kuhn, Loeb & Co.*, nine to ten on *Amsterdamer und Oppenheimer Juden*, eleven on *Französische Finanzjuden*, twelve on *Tschechoslowakische Finanzjuden*, fourteen on *Rumänische Finanzjuden*, fifteen on *Lessing und Moses Mendelssohn und das Bankhaus Mendelssohn & Co.*, seventeen on Polnische Finanzjuden, eighteen on *Schwedische Finanzjuden*, nineteen on *Holländische und belgische Finanzjuden*, twenty on *Frankfurter Finanzjuden und die I.G. Farben*, twenty-one to twenty-three on *Englische Finanzjuden*, thirty-four to thirty-eight and forty-three to forty-four on *Tshechische Finanzjuden* and thirty-nine to forty-two on *Ungarische Finanzjuden*. In addition, he published, in Halle, a similar work on *Amerikanische Finanzjuden* (1936).

15 See below p.120.

16 "nicht mehr zeitgemäßen Kampfmethoden, die sogar von den Engländern in jüngster Zeit zum Zwecke der Gegenpropaganda ausgeschlachtet wurden" (see Gerd Simon, "Chronologie, Pudor, Heinrich", http://homepages.uni-tuebingen.de/gerd.simon/ChrPudor.pdf, p.19f.)

Feder's treatise on national economy, like Rudolf Jung's, is remarkable for its strong moral foundation and its formulation of National Socialism as a movement for social justice as well as for national regeneration. Unlike capitalism with its "soul-destroying materialistic spirit of egoism and avarice with all its concomitant corrupting manifestations in all fields of our public, economic and cultural life" (p.57)[17] and unlike Marxism, which insists that everything should belong to the One, which might be either the State or Mammon controlling it, National Socialism wishes to revert to the mediaeval and Prussian dictum of *suum cuique*, 'to each his own', whereby each person will earn as much as he deserves according to his performance of work, with the fullest possible responsibility, as a duty. Economically, this moral doctrine is translated into the doctrine of serving "the public interest" before self-interest. Not profitability but fulfilment of demand is the National Socialistic basis of the economy.

Unlike Marxism, National Socialism will not prohibit private property but respect it as the privilege of the creative and productive Aryan man. On the other hand, the mobile Jewish mind has no deep connection with the land but rather exploits the productions and property of the natives financially through all sorts of legal claims, bonds and mortgages, whereby "property" is turned into a profitable "possession" (p.30). In order to counter these avaricious strategies of the Jews, the National Socialist state will enforce limitations on the right to property, personal or commercial, so that in all cases the welfare of the whole, the nation, rather than of individuals will be first served. In Feder's discussion of the party's programme in Part II, we note that, since the social policy is "the welfare of the whole", the financial policy of the National Socialist state is accordingly directed against those financial powers who tend to develop "a state within the state" (p.63). As he puts it:

> In the last and deepest analysis, it is a matter of the battle of two world-views that are expressed through two fundamentally different intellectual structures – the productive and creative spirit and the mobile avaricious spirit. The creative spirit rooted in the soil and yet again overcoming the world in metaphysical experience finds its principal representatives in Aryan man – the avaricious, rootless commercial and materialistic spirit directed purely to the this-worldly finds its principal representative in the Jew (p.58).

The strength of Germany before the war was due to its unity under

---

17   All page-references are to the present edition.

The German State on a National and Socialist Foundation

Bismarck and its efficient industrial sector. This advantage was undermined by the dependence of the economy on the credit system of the banks and "the inventors and bearers of the modern credit system" are the Jews (p.63). The mediaeval system of credit was based on the belief ("credo") of the creditor that his money could be used to greater economic advantage by the debtor whereby the debtor, if successful in his enterprise, may return a share of his profits in gratitude to the creditor. Standardised interest, on the other hand, was forbidden by the Church as usury (p.78). Feder advocates a return to the conception of money as a token of "performed work" or of a product so that money cannot, independently of any work, be hoarded for the purpose of being lent out later at interest.

Feder further points out that it is the stock-market that lies at the basis of the alienation of capital from work:

> Anonymisation – the depersonalisation of our economy through the stock-marketable form of the public limited company – has to a certain degree separated capital from work, the share-holder knows in the rarest instances something of his factory, he has only the one-sided interest in the profitability of his money when he has invested it in the form of shares (p.64)

Apart from the indifference of the shareholder to the quality of the goods produced by the company in which he invests, the market in general has diverted production from its legitimate task of fulfilling real needs to that of stirring up - through the Jewish market-crier's technique of advertising - artificial needs among the public that will bring in greater profits. This fundamental transformation of national economics has been supported in academic circles by Jewish scholars who restrict their economic analyses to descriptions of the current economic system rather than investigating its social and political legitimacy. This sort of intellectual subversion is further continued by the Jewish intelligentsia in the fields of art, entertainment and the press.

The major source of the current distress of Germany is indeed the interest owed to large loan capital. The burden of interest has indebted entire nations to international high finance and forced them to become interest-collectors for the latter which they do by taxing the working people ever harder. Feder rightly calls this false economic process an "international fraud" (p.91). The power of international finance has however grown so great that it was able to encircle Germany as soon as it perceived that its currency was rising in strength and independence. Once they succeeded in militarily defeating Germany, the international financial powers then enforced further enormous debt burdens on it through the Treaty of Versailles. Feder therefore proposes the cancellation of the payment of the interest on these debts to the Allies (p.159). Indeed, the remedy to the interest burdens of all nations to international finance is the legal abolition of interest (p.155). And this is simultaneously the solution to the Jewish question itself:

> The solution of the interest problem is the solution of the Jewish question. The solution of the interest problem in the sense of our explanations is the breaking of the Jewish world-rule, because it smashes the power of world Jewry – its financial power.

The fullest representation of the socio-economic interests of a nation should be the state, and its industries should be models of efficiency and commercial success. One example of such an industry in Germany is indeed the transport industry and especially the German railways. Unlike Bolshevism, which seeks to control all production, the National Socialist state will, through the establishment of storage and distribution cooperatives under state supervision (p.35), remove only the avaricious interference of private commerce between production and consumption. As the means of exchange necessary for the exchange of goods, money will be under the control of the state through a nationalised state bank.

Instead of borrowing money from private banks, the state should, in the case of all large public works projects, finance the latter though the issuance of interest-free notes of its own. The Reichsbank's sovereignty of issuing notes must be regained through nationalisation (p.102). Freed of interest-burdens to banks, the state will ultimately be able to operate in a mostly tax-free manner (Ch.22, 'The state without taxes'). Taxes will be restricted to the coverage of non-productive tasks such as the administration of justice, the police system, medical and educational systems, if the commercial enterprises of the state such as the railways post and telegraph, mining and forestry do not present surpluses wherewith to pay for these tasks (p.151). International transactions should be conducted through a clearing system rather like that of the international postal union "without the international finance benefiting two or three times in all these simple mercantile operations and becoming big and fat at the cost of the productive nations" (p.127).

The German State on a National and Socialist Foundation

But the state must be powerful if it is to effect any reforms. Unfortunately, the Weimar Republic has abjectly accepted the monstrous burden of guilt after the war with the result that "the members of the Chosen People can, on these reparations, forever lead a glamorous work-free life in all the countries of the world at the cost of German work." (p.38). The crisis faced by Germany after the war was facilitated by parliamentarianism and Mammonism. The "great democratic lie of the capacity of the people for self-government" is to be combated along with the real capitalistic rulers of democracies. Marxism likewise is a sham socialist system that employs the dissatisfaction of those exploited by Mammonism for the benefit of the "handlers for international capital" in order to "divert from themselves the hatred of the exploited" (p.48).

The majority of the principal Marxists as well as Mammonists are Jews, and so "The Jewish question is becoming a world-question on whose solution the welfare and woe of the nations will be dependent" (p.48). The solution of this question cannot be through violence since "indeed one cannot kill the plague bacillus individually, one can only eradicate it by cutting off its life necessities from it" (p.49). A suggestion of what might be done to reduce their ill-earned gains is contained in point 17 of the party's programme which envisages creation of legal possibilities of confiscating if necessary land that was acquired in an illegal way or not administered according to the viewpoint of the welfare of the people. This is directed thus mainly against the Jewish land speculation companies (p.82)

Further, a removal of Jews from all public positions will cause no difficulty to the nation since "the real vitally important productive activity in industry and agriculture, in the professions and administration, is almost entirely free of Jews" (p.67). Concomitant with the removal of Jews from the "national body" is the enforcement of new citizenship laws whereby the citizenship rights will be "acquired" by the citizens and not merely granted to them. Thus only those who pledge themselves to the German community and culture and do not continue an adherence to another nation can obtain these rights (p.67).

The National Socialist state will be a strong state that includes all the German tribes and its power will be concentrated in a strong leader, or autocrat, who embodies "the highest responsibility" (p.26)[18] since

---

18   The "Führer principle" was championed also by Rudolf Jung in his Nationale

the German people have traditionally wanted a strong leader, and monarchs are not always to be relied upon. The leader of the National Socialist state, on the other hand, is not envisaged as a permanent ruler but one chosen only for the re-establishment of order and prosperity of a debilitated nation. After he has accomplished his goals he may step aside to let other rulers take his place under the constitution. Indeed, the National Socialist state may be characterised as a constitutional autocracy (p.43). The constitutional aspect of the state will be used especially to ensure an effective labour law and social insurance (p.55). Obviously, in a German national state, no members of foreign races can assume the leadership of state affairs (p.53).

Feder is aware of the adverse reaction of the international financiers to such autarkic measures but he believes that a transformation of interest-bearing bonds into interest-free bank assets or postal cheque accounts (p.121) wherewith foreign creditors can be paid will avert the wrath of the latter. He also suggests that boycotts can be overcome through transactions with neutral countries. As for military action, he believes that it is not likely to be pursued by the foreign creditor nations since if the German people saw the French or Jewish tax collector sitting in every tax- and pension office, and if the best cows were taken from the stalls of the farmers by these foreign oppressors – then the anger and indignation would perhaps become soon so strong that one night would sweep the foreign spectre away with a bloody broom and free Germany. (p.162)

We see that, in spite of the lucidity of his economic doctrines, Feder rather underestimated the unforgiving nature of the Mammon that he was striving against. In keeping with Feder's doctrines, the Nationalist Socialist state officially cancelled the war debt to the Allied nations and sought, from 1933 on, to combat the cumulative deflation by the creation of money and work.[19] Work was created by increasing public works activity, such as notably the building of super- highways, and other construction and agricultural projects. These projects were financed, as Feder had recommended, by the issuance of government bills.[20] The production of armaments especially was spurred by the

---

Sozialismus, p.177f.

19 See G. Senft, "Anti-Kapitalismus von Rechts? - Eine Abrechnung mit Gottfried Feders 'Brechung der Zinsknechtschaft'", *Zeitschrift für Sozialökonomie*, 106 (1995), pp.18-32.

20 According to Henry Liu: "through an independent monetary policy of sovereign credit and a full-employment public-works program, the Third Reich was able to turn a bankrupt Germany, stripped of overseas colonies

use of the so-called 'Mefo' bills - named after Schacht's Metallurgische Forschungsgesellschaft (Mefo), which served as a government holding company.[21] These bills were used by government contractors for payment of their needs and were valid as a form of currency. As a result of these economic strategies, as Overy notes, "the banks increasingly became mere intermediaries, holding government stock and helping in the job of keeping bills circulating in the way that the government wanted."[22] Tax levels were simultaneously reduced for farmers, small businesses and heavy industry through the "remission of taxes already paid".[23] However, Hitler was also dependent in his ambitious rearmament plans on foreign finance, which certainly would not have accepted Feder's insistence on an abolition of interest.[24]

The National Socialist economy was an increasingly state-controlled one that sought to avoid inflation by controlling prices and wages and foreign trade. Autarkic restrictions on imports were offset by bilateral barter agreements. Whether the war that began two years after the 1937 edition of Feder's work was, as Feder's view of the role of international finance in the first World War would suggest, another effort to punish Germany's financial independence under National Socialism or whether it was indeed secretly willed by the international financiers for their own geopolitical ends, the increasing losses suffered by Germany in the course of it certainly provoked Hitler into attempting to "sweep the foreign spectre away with a bloody broom", as Feder had predicted.

But neither Feder nor Hitler may have foreseen the severity of the revenge - more cruel since more lasting than that after the first World

---

it could exploit, into the strongest economy in Europe within four years, even before armament spending began" (Henry C.K. Liu, "Nazism and the German economic miracle," *Asia Times Online*, 24 May 2005, http://www.atimes.com/atimes/Global_Economy/GE24Dj01.html).

21 Hitler's eagerness to rearm Germany is not surprising in the light of the eastern expansionist and anti-Bolshevist foreign political aims outlined by him already in *Mein Kampf*, Vol.II, Ch.14.

22 R.J. Overy, *The Nazi Economic Recovery 1932-1938*, Cambridge: Cambridge University Press, 1996, p.43.

23 *Ibid.*, p.38.

24 See the web-log by "Scanners", "Gottfried Feder und das zinslose Geld", http://www.utopia.de/blog/umweltpolitik/gottfried-feder-und-das-zinslose. The western financial powers may have partly supported Hitler's effort to check the westward spread of Bolshevism. For American involvement in National Socialist finance, for example, see Anthony C. Sutton, *Wall Street and the rise of Hitler*, Sudbury: Bloomfield Books, 1976.

Preface

War - that the international Jewish interests would take on Germany after its defeat in 1945. While Feder hoped that other nations of the world will also eventually follow the German example and "mankind, freed of the Jewish oppression, will experience an age of unprecedented prosperity – and, above all, Germany - the heart of the world", the opposite of that indeed has occurred, since most of Europe has been turned into "a slave, fellaheen, bondman and servant of the all-Jewish world-power" (p.62). And the heart of Germany itself, drained by a tyrannical psychological control of its population, has virtually stopped beating.

Preface to the Fifth Edition

Here my work, *The German State on a national and socialist foundation*, appears within the series of the "National Socialist Library". The text has remained essentially and basically unchanged but the passages that referred to circumstances of the time when this work appeared (1923) and borrowed examples therefrom were deleted and the explanations of the Jewish question shortened since a special work will be dedicated to the latter.

The new edition should especially give evidence of the fact that nothing in the least was changed in the basic programme.

Gottfried Feder

Murnau, October 1931

Foreword by Adolf Hitler

Every great idea needs two things, the will to power and clear goals. The will to power, to liberation, lies glowing and strong in our hearts, Gottfried Feder has in his book, *The German State On A National And Socialist Foundation*, presented our goals clearly and simply and in a way understandable to everybody. In it the hope and longing of millions has found a form and powerful expression. The literature of our movement has in it obtained its catechism.

Adolf Hitler

Munich, 8 November 1923.

Blessed are the people to whom a stark necessity imposes a lofty political idea which, being great and simple, forces every other idea of the age into its service. - Heinrich von Treitschke

Introduction to the First Edition

We look into the future full of strong hope and longing. Germany will live, Germany cannot go down. Germany is shaken as if by the overpowering birth-pangs of a new age. The horrid shackles of self-guilt, as well as the foreign tormentors, will fall away and will be shaken off with a powerful shrug, and Germany will march at the head of the nations.

If so much suffering and distress were not connected with the collapse and downfall we would be able to participate with a certain feeling of happiness in the days of creation of a new age. If we cast our glance upon the degradations of the day, on the confusion of the present, we see everywhere a powerful will, serious work, inspired intuition. The German soul moves its wings to a new high flight.

The tasks today are powerful, greater and harder than ever in the so painful history of the Germans.

So it is necessary to solve the twofold task – not just to "rebuild" the state and economy - but to give them a new form. And a new form thereby also for the cultural and intellectual life of our people.

The old German longing for a united Germany must finally become a reality, a new economic law will arise and sweep away the nightmarish form of interest capitalistic economics.

So comprehensive and overpowering are the tasks that await us. Grave and admonishing stands the spirit of the past behind us; filled with awe before that which has occurred historically, on the solid ground of the best German tradition, based on the earliest Aryan wisdom, the people and the state, economics and culture must be created anew.

Here the workers must be conscious of their enormous responsibility, indeed they are borne by the hope of the entire nation - towards freedom!

But the National Socialist idea is much more than only a return or a detour into old ancestral customs, it breaks the chains of the Marxist state and economic form, it, as the first and most determined idea, consciously fights the hardest battle against the Mammonistic powers, against the world-encompassing power of the all-Jewish imperialism, against the spirit of rapacity, selfishness and indifference.

Introduction to the First Edition

This universal and great German freedom movement finds its most powerful, strong-willed and goal-conscious campaigner in the National Socialist German Workers' Party. The party has outlined its goals in a short programme that summarises in a pithy way the fundamental demands of the movement in 25 clauses. Alfred Rosenberg, the chief editor of the Nationalist Observer,[25] the polemical organ of the National Socialist movement of Greater Germany, has, in a manner worthy of thanks, explained the programme points individually in a short work.[26] On the basis of this work it is at least possible to say to friends and enemies what the National Socialist German Workers' Party wants. On the other hand, there is lacking in the literature of National Socialism a comprehensive work that would give an account of the political and economic ideas from which National Socialism proceeds, what paths it intends to forge with regard to national politics in order to arrive at its final goal, that of the National Socialist German state, the state of work and performance. The present work wishes to fulfil this task. We will therefore have to illumine the point of departure, the way and the goal of National Socialism, we shall show wherein the German National Socialist state will essentially differ from the existing state, which fields will remain essentially untouched, on which fields there will be substantial reforms, and where essentially new paths will have to be entered upon.

We shall have to seek and reveal new ways for public life, especially for the national financial policy, for the treatment of the racial question and the questions connected with it. We shall further have to fundamentally deal with hostile objections, distortions and lies that have already become loud.

The task that we have set to ourselves is extremely great and yet only a small part of the entire scope of Germany's renewal. All effort would be in vain if a determinedness unto death and the unrestrained will of a leader did not work for the efficacy of the ideas. The strongest will would be wasted uselessly if we did not bear in our hearts unshakeably a clear image of what this German state – Germany, the land of our fathers and children - should look like in accordance with our will – after our victory!

---

25 [The *Völkischer Beobachter* was bought in 1920 by the NSDAP as the organ of the party and edited by Dietrich Eckart until his death in 1923, when it was led by Alfred Rosenberg.]

26 [Rosenberg first published his *Wesen, Grundsätze und Ziele der Nationalsozialistischen Deutschen Arbeiterpartei. Das Programm der Bewegung* in 1923.]

I. The Foundations

The Moral Foundations

The foundation of National Socialist statecraft is complete responsibility with regard to the people and with regard to oneself.

"Public interest before self-interest" is the first law of National Socialism.

It may seem strange that such a principle must be generally established for a state, for we recognise from history periods in which the welfare of the whole was in the mind of the rulers as the foundation of their state leadership. If it is necessary today to set this principle before all other considerations, this is only the expression of the fact that the present-day public conditions are anything but the expression of this sole correct political sentiment. We see equally in this first principle how intimately morality and economics are involved with each other.

Public interest before self-interest is first a moral demand. But it expresses at the same time with excellent linguistic clarity the hierarchical ordering between the welfare of the whole and the justified striving of the individual for personal acquisition and property. This National Socialist principle therefore in no way excludes private property. On the contrary: National Socialism acknowledges fully and completely the significance of property. It knows that personal property and a right to dispose of an acquisition freely is the foundation of every economics and, beyond that, of every higher culture; but National Socialism has recognised equally that for the acknowledgement of private property it is necessary to draw quite definite limits, that is, where property becomes a mere instrument of power and is applied in an exploitative way against the welfare of the whole.

There is perhaps hardly one seriously thinking person who would like to contradict this first principle in this general form. The difficulty will lie in the right assessment of public interests against those of the individual private person. In spite of the doubtlessly existing agreement that the considerations of the public interest have to go before the

I. The Foundations

private interests, remarkably there has been, according to the legal ideas valid among us, precisely with regard to the form of the use of property, no moral limitation determined beyond the criminal. It is, to be sure, forbidden to act with violence against one's fellow man (extortion – murder – manslaughter – betrayal and illegitimate enrichment, etc.), but it has never and nowhere been forbidden to pile up immeasurable wealth and to make use of the often quite dubious banking and stock-exchange technical means therein. Further, the law gives every creditor the right to ruthlessly deprive a delinquent debtor of his home and possessions when adverse conditions – illness, death, malformation, bad harvests and famine - make the fulfilment of incurred obligations impossible. Every experienced judge can relate numberless cases in which our rigid law has destroyed economic existences in cases in which every healthy sense of justice has revolted against delivering a hardworking, diligent man who has, however, been dogged by bad luck temporarily to the brutal pressure and grasp of the creditor.

The limitless acknowledgement of personal right to property and legal claims on the whole must logically lead to the damaging of the public interest through the selfish exploitation of this basically inverted anti-social legal idea in opposition to our state principle "Public interest before self-interest".

In contrast to the false fundamental formulation ruling among us, the capitalistic, is the other extreme, the Marxist idea of the state and economics. The fundamental idea of this economic form is the denial of private property. The Marxist doctrine goes so far as to explain property directly as "theft" (Proudhon).[27] It demands, in the foreign jargon that is so unclear especially to German proletarians, the "expropriation of the expropriators".[28] - in other words, the dispossession of property! This state-, people-, culture- and economy destroying doctrine has found its extreme but logical realisation in Russian Bolshevism. In its economic aspect this extreme can be summarised in the sentence: "Everything belongs to everybody".

We have here to do with a depersonalisation of property, with a transfer of all property to the anonymous property of the whole.

---

27 [Pierre Joseph Proudhon (1809-1865) declared in his 1840 work *Qu'est-ce que la propriété?* that *la propriété c'est le vol.*]

28 [This phrase, borrowed from the French "l'expropriation des expropriateurs", is used by Marx in *Das Kapital*, I, Ch.24: "The final hour of private property strikes .The expropriators are expropriated".]

The German State on a National and Socialist Foundation

The extreme still ruling among us of an unlimited right to property, on the other hand, has led us already to the last step before the temple of the god Mammon, on whose door stands in golden letters: "Everything belongs to the One". Even this frightening economic form must equally lead to a depersonalisation of property – only in another way – in that, finally, all of working mankind is here pressed into a frightful debt slavery to an anonymous financial power.

In starkest contrast to the just described economic extremes of Marxist socialism and high capitalist Mammonism of the western democrats, the economic ideal of National Socialism demands the realisation of the principle, "To each his own".

Precisely in this principle are morality and economics once again most intimately interconnected. The removal of moral principles from the commercial life is indeed so characteristic of the present-day economy in which just the superior power of greater possession, greater cunning, the art of avoiding the state authority even in the most hazardous dealings, tips the balance. A glance at the thousands of mostly dark existences that conduct their mischief in all big cities, who dispose of fantastic sums, a glance at the several suits that come to a trial in spite of all the resistance of the participants, shows us how frightfully depraved the present-day commercial morality is. Let us consider, in contrast to that, the frightful misery in the circles of the middle-class and of the married working people who can no longer pay for milk and bread for their infants and growing children, let us be clear that generally in many, many cases with honourable work hardly the basic necessities for life can be earned, especially when there are children to be looked after and raised. The distress of the intellectual and free professions exceeds all measure; artists of the very first rank, especially when their orientation does not correspond to the Jewish orientation of taste that rules today, are flatly delivered to hunger; genuine German poems can achieve no public performance. But quite indescribable is the distress of those who have, through the mismanagement of the state with regard to financial policy, been cheated of their savings, the small capital pensioners and retirees, the war disabled, those forced to charity help, as well as all those who have relied on the certainty of public bonds as well as on the stability of our national currency and the gold coverage of the mark.

Such a condition is a decomposition of the economy – anarchy. Industriousness is repaid with insufficient remuneration, laziness is rewarded, honourable trade suffers distress, unhealthy trade,

I. The Foundations

intermediary trade, profiteering prosper best of all. The more superior in cultural aspects a production is so much the worse is the remuneration that can be obtained. Trust is repaid with betrayal, and indeed by the state, which should be the protector of law and justice, the attorney of public morality.

We do not at all need any more to point to the corruption in public life, the judaisation and the impoverishment of the press and the miserably powerless and unworthy leadership of our foreign policy to indicate the extreme debasement of our public life and our economic morality.

Against this materialistic impoverishment and contamination of the public life the National Socialist idea of the state sets the long tested principle of state and economy: "To each his own", but above all "Public interest before self-interest". With the raising of this principle to the guiding principle of the National Socialist state National Socialism binds itself to the best and most glorious periods of German history.

"*Suum cuique*"[29] was already the economic principle of the healthy German early Middle Ages, but especially for a long period it was ensured through the ordering of the guilds that to each was allotted his own. The commonalty of work between master and apprentice for half or a third of a penny at least ensured the worker his income, better work and performance found their acknowledgement and their reward and, in cases of outstanding performance, fame and rich earnings.

"Suum cuique" adorns also the highest Prussian order, the Order of the Black Eagle, though here in the special sense that to special merit is due its crown. Precisely this interpretation corresponds quite especially to National Socialism – not so much because it is here a matter of courtly decoration pieces or the one-sided honouring of military service but because the moral content of the rewarded fulfilment of duty with regard to the state and people finds its expression therein, a fulfilment of duty which is done selflessly without design and without a previous regard for clinking wages, with a relegation of personal interests to the background, born of an inner compelling feeling of responsibility towards the state and the people.

---

29   [To each his own]

The German State on a National and Socialist Foundation

We National Socialists extend this principle also in the other direction, we add to the "to each his own" of the German Middle Ages and to the idea of "To merit its crown" of Friedrich's state, with greatest emphasis: "To the criminal his punishment!". To each his own, to merit its crown, to every orderly and honourable work its adequate payment, to every special performance its higher remuneration, to every poor person and every person who has fallen innocently into distress sufficient help from public funds, but equally to all those who act against public morality and economic respectability – the deserved punishment.

However, we stress that it does not in any way lie within the scope of duties of the National Socialist state to supervise the state citizen individually in economic matters, that the economy prospers best free as far as possible from bureaucratic tutelage. We know also that a decrease of risk in the case of every individual state citizen through the state – rather in the sense of Naumann's "risk-free man", that is, of a man for whose basic existence the state should provide – would achieve precisely the opposite of that which Naumann expected of it.[30] The duty of the state must be limited to creating the preconditions for an economy which holds itself as free as possible from the frightful usurious phenomena which we know in the present-day interest capitalistic state.

The welfare of the state must therefore become once again the highest law, the efficiency of the state must set the principle "Public interest before self-interest" before all other considerations.

Now this principle however makes necessary among the statesmen, the state employees and those who stand in outstanding positions in the public life, a characteristic that has today almost completely disappeared from government and public life – responsibility.

Our entire public life stands today directly under the sign of irresponsibility. The delegates are not responsible for – one says "immune to" - what they do and speak in parliament. A desperate term when one remembers that this expression is taken from medicine in which it is said that a body is already so saturated with poisons that

---

30 [Friedrich Naumann (1860-1919) was a Protestant theologian and liberal politician who founded the Nationalsozialen Verein in 1896 and propagated a form of social liberalism through his journal *Die Hilfe*. After the first World War, Naumann became the first chairman of the Deutsche Demokratische Partei.(DDP).]

I. The Foundations

newly infused poisons harm the body much less or not at all whereas a healthy body would die of them. The fractions are not responsible for the decisions of the majority, the ministers are not responsible for the discharge of their office for they are only functionaries of the parties that participate precisely in the formation of a government. If something goes wrong, the people indeed suffer the worst damages, but the so-called responsible minister is only replaced by another equally irresponsible party functionary. Of real responsibility there is no mention.

Already the appeal to the Almighty in the age of the divine right of kings was unfortunately only too often a quite special form of the irresponsibility of the ruling lords – (rare exceptions for whom the responsibility to their god was synonymous with their feeling of responsibility towards their people are expressly acknowledged). In general, however, this dear god was always, in the final analysis, only a comfortable protective shield behind which could hide, on the step-ladder of the official responsible only to his superior, of the minister responsible only to his king and of the ruler responsible only to his god, the most incredible irresponsibility of the ruling class and its representatives with regard to the actual life-necessities of the people.

National Socialism will have to radically clear away this state sanctioned irresponsibility.

'Highest responsibility' will stand in iron letters over the entrance gate to the National Socialist state. One who has the honour to stand in a leading position for the interests of a great people cannot be reminded strongly enough of his responsibility. Indeed, only he can be a leader who bears this deepest feeling of responsibility in his breast. For all state employees and for those who stand in public life this responsibility is to be especially stipulated and also carried out with ruthless strictness. Only in this way can a recovery actually be compelled, so to speak. Only in this way can the most precious thing be revived and grow that may allow the leader and the people once again to become a real national and historical community – trust. And from trust then can the faith grow once again which, with the responsibility of the leader, will bring forth a recovery and renewal of Germany, a reawakening of the German soul, in a nationalist state of work and performance in which each will find his own.

The Economic Foundations

In a healthy economic body morality and national economy cannot be separated. Otherwise the economy suffers in the most severe manner, especially with respect to the most honourable task of every economy – the fulfilment of demand. Without faith in commerce, without industriousness, without the loyalty of the officials and workers no work can prosper. Efficiency, justice, entrepreneurial spirit, energy, mutual trust between all taking part in an economic task are the indispensable preconditions for the prospering of every economy. All these things need to be said only to be acknowledged in their exceptional significance. Everybody who has had to be economically active in the present and the recent past knows to what extent these fine things are lacking today. And who finally suffers the damages of the salvation doctrines of Marxism and its operational methods, the strikes, sabotage and negligent and slovenly work? - But in the end only the population itself which, through such state- and people-disintegrating doctrines, lost all feeling of community and sees its most important work in class-struggle. Therefore to this quarter must also be directed the complaints which ring out especially from the nationalist camps that we are no longer a people, that we should first become a people once again if we wished to reacquire our lost position of power and international standing.

These complaints are justified, but with complaints one does not go forward. Marxism did not hesitate to realise its economic and political ideal when it had the power to do so, it did not shy away from brutal suppression of dissidents: in Russia it silenced its enemies forever by slaughtering the entire bourgeois intelligentsia, among us through the laws for the protection of the republic.[31] The acquisition of political power is obviously the precondition of every economic or national political reform. That we know as well as the Communists and the Social Democrats, but we want political power not for its own sake, not to exploit the acquired position of power against a certain class but to create the preconditions for an economic peace among the national comrades bound together into a work community. The fulfilment of demand[32] is the task of the national economy – not profitability,

---

31   [Post-war Germany has a similar law, the Federal Law for the Protection of the Constitution (Bundesverfassungsschutzgesetz), which was passed in 1950.]

32   By fulfilment of demand is to be understood the satisfaction, through affordable prices, of the life necessities of the totality of all those bound together into a national community.

I. The Foundations

which is today almost solely decisive in the production of goods. With this fundamental attitude of National Socialism we enter in definite opposition to the basic economic ideas of the capitalist state. Not what was necessary was produced in the first place but what was profitable. Any thing that did not promise to yield sufficient interests and dividends was from the start not taken up. As an especially clear example of the profitability madness of the present interest capitalistic economy may serve the fact that housing construction, in spite of the frightful need for housing – thus in spite of the most urgent need – is simply not carried out because it is not profitable! That housing construction considered in a national political way in a higher sense would indeed be profitable requires in this place no further explanation but is straightaway clear from what has been said especially with regard to the social tasks of the state. Further, if the people hunger and freeze, then a capitalist economy directed to profit does not in any way see its duty in fulfilling this need through the production of cheap and good shoes, clothes and underwear, etc., for with the lowered purchasing capacity of the population this is not "profitable". On the other hand, the luxuries industry in all fields is fully busy, for never before was effortlessly acquired wealth so eager to surround itself with sheer luxury as today. But the capitalist idea of profitability actually becomes an economic nonsense in the branches of our economy that today rule everything, in the banking and stock-exchange system.

The fact of the ruling position of the banks proves most strikingly the economic senselessness of the capitalist idea. With the "productions" of the banks and stock-exchanges never yet has a child been fed, never yet has a freezing person been clothed, in general never has even the smallest requirement that is necessary for life been supplied. This statement is not at all a demagogic catchphrase, it does not even include the dispensability of the institutions of monetary transactions, it only shows with all clarity what an enormous difference there exists between a really national economic fulfilment of demand, such as National Socialist wishes, and a completely private-capitalistically oriented profit-based economy.

Even the National Socialist state will have its banks and other financial institutions, but they will no longer be the rulers of the national economy but their servants, money will no longer be the lord of the state and people but only the necessary aid for the exchange of goods. We know precisely that this battle against the bank- and stock-exchange capital will mean the hardest battle for the National Socialist movement because today the most enormous plenitude of power that the globe has ever borne is concentrated in the bank- and stock-exchange capital. Here it is a question of a life and death battle for power, this the opponent knows better than most of our friends and followers. This battle will be so much more difficult in that entire sections of the population are still caught in the profitability madness.

A fundamental question which should be answered in this place once again with all clarity is the question how National Socialism basically stands in relation to property. From the fundamental observations of the first chapter and especially from the fundamental opposition described there to Marxist Socialism there results with natural consequence for National Socialism the fundamental acknowledgement of property. This acknowledgement of private property is too deeply anchored in Aryan life. The creative mind which recognises the environment, which contemplates the environment in order to create and form therefrom its world, the creative man who wrests its fruits from the earth through hard work, who settles down, builds for himself homes and cities, who, having become settled and rooted in the circle of his kinsmen, his racial comrades, the man who then proceeds on such an infrastructure rooted in the soil to higher culture and creates for himself his - the - world in a higher intellectual sense, in the fields of philosophy, poetry, music, art and sculpture – this man certainly cannot conceive of it differently than that the works of his hand, which have been born out of his own, are also his property. From this knowledge of the creative man arises directly the respect for the property of others, and law arises.

In fundamental and irreconcilable opposition to the creative mind stands the avaricious thieving mind of other men disposed differently, who have never known the breath of creation, who move restlessly from place to place, who could never put down roots anywhere, who did not rise expansively, and from the soil, in a long development to ever higher culture but, with their restlessly moving mind and with their money, moved from country to country, when they had "grazed" the individual cities or tracts of land. Even in the fields of the creative nations the Jew essentially stood quite far removed from the actual productions, we do not know the Jew as a farmer, not as tradesmen, not as engineers or master-builders, not as factory- and wage workers, and true creative genius is foreign to him even in the fine arts and in the sciences. The moving mind begins its characteristic activity only where a work has been created

I. The Foundations

by a creative hand, an object has been produced, there the avaricious mind knows to procure these goods for itself and to move them to its pecuniary advantage. Not to supply the national economic demand but to strike as high a profit as possible for itself from this traffic of production to consumption it set itself up between producer and consumer – the trader arose. Today the trader and money-changer has become the board of directors and banking lord. The economy of the entire world has been turned upside down in the most senseless manner. The clever, inventive, daring, creative and productive mind no longer rules; the crooked mind, incapable of creating anything of its own, exploitative and avaricious, rules. Money rules over work and blood.

The moving mind of the Jew has been able to make everything mobile, even the land through mortgages, the largest long-established industries through anonymisation and through the stock company, and, through the state bond economy, international capital has even separated the governments from their peoples. Today the governments are all dependent on large loan capital and in relation to their peoples they are only the interest collectors for their anonymous lords in Wall Street, the City of London and Paris.

These brief observations have shown us the deepest secret of the irreconcilable opposition between creative peoples and the avaricious Jew. *"The Aryan creates, the Jew grabs the world for himself"*.

Here it may be briefly added further that there exists a very fine difference between property and possession. Possession need not at all necessarily be property, possession cannot be self-created. In the case of a possession the origin of the possession is not questioned. The Jew has seized possession of the property of the Aryan peoples and now rules the creators through his financial power. This abstracted form of property in the form of legal claims, bonds, mortgages, etc. has made the entire world today subject through interest to capital. The interest capitalistic economic form generally knows no limits of possession, it suffers entire nations with all their work to become subject to interest to a handful of bank- and stock-exchange magnates.

Against this not a little frightening interest-capitalistic robber economy National Socialism sets the limitation of the right to property. The principle for this limitation lies in the sentence: "Public interest before self-interest". That this limit for property moreover

The German State on a National and Socialist Foundation

can be raised very high emerges from the fact that National Socialism will not in any way reject even the largest industrial works, so long as they remain in the private possession of the creators (we think of Krupp, Mannesmann, Thyssen, etc.), as contradicting the interests of the whole, especially when the owners of these large works have a feel for and understanding of social questions and are able to find the right limits between appropriate self-gain from production, an adequate pricing for the sales and the fulfilment of demand of the national economy, and a corresponding and worthy form of participation of the workforce in the revenues of the works.

Here we come to brief fundamental observations on the external forms of production. The powerfully rising German economy before the war was distinguished by a very fortunate mixture of big-, medium- and small businesses. Now, in general, in the tendency to big business there indeed lies a danger for the national economy insofar as the next step above the big business, the syndicate, no longer serves the fulfilment of demand but the high capitalistic interests of the domination of the market and of the dictatorship of prices. Nevertheless it is plainly conceded that certain industries can work only as big businesses. This applies to those industrial branches that we generally designate as heavy industries.

Without wishing to go into details at this point it may be basically stated that the National Socialist state has no reason to strive for fundamental changes in these external forms of the economy. National Socialism rejects all sorts of "socialisation or nationalisation" in the Marxist sense. Our economic ideal demands as large a number of economically free existences precisely in the medium and small businesses. We know that only the free and independent men who can freely dispose of their work and their work income are filled with a serious feeling of responsibility with regard to their work, that only on this soil do powerful personalities arise and that only on the soil of freedom and responsibility prospers the sense of the community which unites those bound through common work to a community of life and destiny and therewith makes them a free, self-conscious nation. Only on such a soil can the welfare of the individual be united with the welfare of the whole.

I. The Foundations

On the Boundaries of the State and the Economy

Manchesterism[33] and State Socialism are the polar opposites when it comes to establishing the limits which the state must observe in its intervention in the economy. The first doctrine demands as much freedom as possible from every state guardianship, it would like best to see the state relegated to the role of a night-watchman. State Socialism believes that most businesses are best conducted and administered by the state itself. The most extreme forms of socialisation or nationalisation, which is the Russian term for the running of the enterprises by all, have shown to everybody who has observed the Socialist experiments impartially, with conclusive clarity, that such Communistic forms of production are in the long run unfeasible. One who has followed our explanations of the foundations of the economy will be able to recognise without difficulty the inner reasons for this phenomenon. On the one hand, the suppression of the entrepreneurial initiative, the lack of the profit motive, the removal of competition, on the other hand the compulsion to work which was exercised with ruthless force by the Soviets must reduce the advantage of production to a minimum.

The gradual, milder form of "state-control" of businesses as we know it from our German economic life is to be applied successfully to advantage only in different fields of the public economy. In the fields which are conducted in competition with the free economy, especially in the field of large industrial production (coal), the commercial success is strongly limited in comparison to the free economy, which is in a position to take all important decisions more quickly and independently than is necessarily possible in the case of state enterprises. In order to have a right judgement of what businesses are in general suited for state control, we must be clear of what position the state assumes in the total operation of a national economy.

We have explained that National Socialism sees the task of economics in the fulfilment of demand. Producer and consumer, manufacturer and user, are the two chief participants in every economy. Now we know that the use is, in the final analysis, always and everywhere

---

33 [Manchesterism is the school of economic thought that arose in the 19th century in Manchester as a reaction against the protectionist Corn Laws of 1815 and 1846. It advocated free trade and supported the industrialists against the agrarian interests of the landed aristocracy. The principal proponents of this movement were Richard Cobden (1804-1865) and John Bright (1811-1889).]

The German State on a National and Socialist Foundation

purely individual, or expressed very clearly: every piece of bread can indeed be consumed only by one person, clothes are also destined only for personal use, a flat provides at any time a roof only to a small, connected circle, the work-place gives at any time a position to only a perhaps greater but still limited number of work comrades, so we cannot at all speak of a common consumption or use of products. If therefore consumption is, in the final analysis, individual, the same is true also of production, of the production of goods. The more valuable the product of productive work is, the clearer it is that this arises only from a highly personal creative force. For the works of the mind in the fields of science and the fine arts, in the field of technical inventions and discoveries this is immediately clear, but even in the case of assembled work in factory-like enterprises, in which the mechanisation through machines suppresses almost entirely human individual work, it is finally still valid that the pair of shoes that precisely this worker manufactures can be manufactured only by this one and not by another. The quality of the products however sinks with increasing mechanisation. Already in the agricultural business the old rule is valid: "The eye of the lord fattens the cattle", that is, only the personal care of the breeder obtains the highest results.

All attempts of the Communist economy have ended every time in a complete failure. We must therefore declare fundamentally that both consumption and production go against socialisation. Now, as soon as mankind abandoned the original economic forms of individual economy in the family and moved to more complicated economic forms through division of labour and had formed great state communities, there intervened between production and consumption something new – trade and commerce and the financial system.

This very plain economic philosophical observation gives us the clearest evidence of the fields in which the state has to limit its economic activity. It is indeed immediately clear that it is here a question of matters in which every individual is equally interested. And it is only logical that here the state will find its scope of duties as the embodiment of the common interests.

If our economic philosophy is right, the state must have performed something exemplary in one of these fields in case it has tried its hand at one already. This it has also performed in the field of transport. The performances of the German railway authorities before the war were just exemplary, and they are that even today to the extent that the old

I. The Foundations

fidelity to duty and conscientiousness still rule. One also often credits the non-state railway system in America with special perfection; this is also accurate in a certain context insofar as the traffic occurs rather more freely, and many small difficulties which are with us bound to the bureaucratic system could hardly have been avoided. Even the building of locomotives of great dimensions in America evoked astonishment amongst us earlier, but the chief reason for this was that the broader gauge of the American railway network made this indeed more easily possible technically. But this is not an aspect of transport but a technical fact which does not belong to the scope of our observations. On the other hand, much more important for our question is – the security of the transport in the railways. In this field the German railways were constantly aware of this uppermost task of the state transport and can also claim the reputation for itself for having done, technically and organisationally, everything that was possible.

With what irresponsible recklessness the life of the passengers was endangered in this field precisely in the American and French railways emerges from the history of railway accidents on American railways and on French railways before the nationalisation, as long as these served the reckless pursuit of profit of the Paris Rothschilds. - Even here therefore we see once again the fundamental opposition between the capitalistic idea of profitability and the idea of duty of the demand fulfilment economy.

The task of commerce is, in the first place, to serve the national economy through the secure, quick and cheap transfer of goods and persons to the places of use or work. The question of profitability comes only in the second place in a state enterprise, or it is only a question of tariff policy. To commerce belongs naturally also the post and telegraph system. Even here it requires only the honourable memory of the performances of the German post and telegraph administration to show how securely, quickly and reliably this important national economic task was fulfilled by the state.

Trade, on the other hand, has always been considered as the exclusive task of private entrepreneurial initiative. Now, trade cannot be spoken of so unequivocally as the transport system. For a state regulation there comes into consideration from the start only a certain type of goods, indeed mass-consumption goods. As little understanding as one could expect before the war of a state regulation of trade in the most important food products - since the free trade doctrine ruled our national economic way of thought -, so little can one expect today, in view of the shameless usury in the most important food products during the still unforgotten post-war period, that the idea that it is the task of the state to provide for the preparation, transfer and distribution of the most important food products will fall on fertile soil. Exceptionally we do find, even among our antipodes in the economic field, the Bolshevists, attempts to solve this problem, that is, through the state control of production and its distribution. What is wrong there, as we have already shown, is wanting to conduct the production or to understand it always in a state-controlled way. On the other hand, the right distribution of the production is doubtless an especially important state task.

It is remarkable that in Russia the only bourgeois organisations that have remained preserved were the agricultural production and consumer cooperatives, thus, in other words, those organisations that had precisely set themselves the task of storing and collecting the most important food products in the common interest and, on the other hand, of supplying the consumer in the common interest. A survey of our German economic life shows us now that, even among us, this idea is not completely new but that the cooperative idea has been increasingly taking hold everywhere and therewith creating the preconditions that National Socialism has in mind for the regulation of this extraordinarily important question. The cooperative utilisation of agricultural products ensures, on the one hand, to the farmer the removal of his products at adequate prices, it ensures the cooperative purchase of fertilisers, agricultural implements, etc., and it especially makes attempts to ensure the fulfilment of demand through the establishment of agricultural warehouses. On the other hand, the consumer unions have for their part taken completely practical steps to supply the products to the consumers as directly as possible and above all with the suppression of intermediary trade. A merging of the production cooperatives and the consumer cooperatives under state supervision is destined to solve this question.

Even here the core of the question is once again: Not profitability, but the fulfilment of demand is the first task of the economy.

For trade there remains more than enough to occupy it especially in all the fields where the personal factor of risk comes into question. For a food product which is secure always, and in all the circumstances of the sales, the factors that characterise the businessman are from the start eliminated.

I. The Foundations

The financial system is the third and most important thing that is to be brought under state regulation. Money is explained by many financial theorists as a means of exchange for the exchange of products; this explanation is indeed not false but also not comprehensive and not clear. Nevertheless this definition expresses the right feeling that money is an aid for the traffic in goods. The fact that the state claims the privilege of coinage for itself already proves that the state considers money as an especially important field of public life. The fact that the state has produced an entire series of sections in the penal code that deal with counterfeiting proves similarly that it is a matter of a public matter of the first importance. In fact the state has also for a long time determined through its own authority what is to be valid as money in public commerce. A special orientation of financial theoreticians - the Chartalists[34] - represents the state theory of money which summarily declares: "Money is what the state declares to be money". Therewith money is entirely separated from the substance of money, and the seal of the state sovereignty is sufficient to make "money" from iron, aluminium, porcelain and, above all, paper. The present teaches us that this theory has in fact become reality. The opponents of these financial theoreticians – the Metallists[35] – cling to the old idea that money must have an inner value, thus must be from precious metal (gold and silver). The relations of the present do not bear this orientation out for, in fact, the state even makes money out of paper, and indeed money with which one can really buy something, even when the banknotes are made of quite worthless paper. But the question of the purchasing power of this money is another story. Here the sinking purchasing power of money that stands in inverse proportion to the swelling amount of paper money seems to prove the Metallists right, for actually the coins of gold and silver have not caused the loss of purchasing power of paper money. But this is due to another reason, namely to the commodity character of gold money. Not because the gold money is real gold does it maintain its purchasing power but because gold money is also a commodity.

The twenty mark coin today derives its purchasing power not at all from the stamped state currency sign '20 Marks' but from its content of the commodity of refined gold..But we cannot linger here longer

---

34 [Chartalists support the use of fiat money or government-issued tokens (Latin: *charta*) as the national currency.]

35 [Metallists hold that money derives its value from precious metals and oppose fiat money as having no intrinsic value.]

The German State on a National and Socialist Foundation

on these financial theoretical controversial questions, we will have to speak at greater length on these questions in the representation of the state financial system according to the reasoning of the National Socialist reform. Here it is a matter of recognising that the financial system, in the case of the question exercising us at the moment about the boundaries of the state and economy, belongs in any case to the fields which, as an eminently important matter of the entire economic life, exactly like commerce and trade in the most important food products, must definitely be subjected to the most careful fiduciary regulation on the part of the state.

The importance of the financial problem in itself requires today no special explanation. The power of the large financial powers ruling everything lies manifest to anyone that wishes to see it. The perspicacious person has already for long recognised that precisely the incompetent, false manner in which the state has positioned itself with regard to the financial system is the basic reason for the present-day catastrophic conditions in the state finances. The fact that most of the so-called state central banks are not at all purely state institutes but stock companies in which the governments have retained for themselves only certain supervisory rights already gives an idea of the muddled conditions in the field of the public financial system. In reality the nationalisation of the central banks, especially the Reichsbank Public Ltd. Co. (!), has virtually meant the transfer of the most important state sovereign rights to private capital. In addition, the large banks and the other financial institutions have become the unrestrained rulers of the entire national economy.

The National Political Foundations

No state without power and, without authority, no government. Nothing is more self-evident, and more immediately obvious to common sense. One must attribute it to the entire neglect of our public thought if, among us in the government circles, one still believes today that one is able to rule at all with a total lack of military and political power.

Power without an instrument of power is unthinkable; political power and military means of power condition each other mutually just as intimately as economy and morality may not be separated. In order to regain lost power there is only the sole means of creating a military instrument of power.

I. The Foundations

How frightfully our poor fatherland has been punished because it has abjured the idea of power and given itself to the pacifistic fanfare we experience now daily and hourly. "To prevent a worse situation" we have ourselves surrendered and destroyed our weapons, "to prevent a worse situation" we have signed the Versailles dictate, "to prevent a worse situation" the Berlin government has said yes and amen to everything that was demanded of us, "to prevent a worse situation" we have allowed every malice, every humiliation, every exploitation to be enacted against us. With this shameless catchword of cowardice and abjectness the German people have been led into ever deeper misery. We fulfilled what was demanded of us, and a minister who wished to be a German, Dr. Rathenau,[36] dared to declare publicly: There is no absolute inability to fulfil, it is only a matter of how deep a people may be allowed to fall into distress!! This means in other words – although the words of Rathenau are already clear enough: the German nation is completely defenceless, it is politically completely powerless, intellectually it has been almost stultified, it can just continue to work. It has allowed itself to be burdened with such a gigantic burden of guilt that the members of the Chosen People can, on these reparations, forever lead a glamorous work-free life in all the countries of the world at the cost of German work. But now there exists the danger that even the enormous workforce of the Germans may break under the fantastic burden. Therefore the Germans must be kept alive constantly through stimulants and precisely in this way be maintained at the limit of their physical performance capacity that they may work summoning all strength always in the deceptive hope that they might one day free themselves from their burdens. "It is only a matter of how deep a people may be allowed to fall into distress!" This was the political sentiment of the Minister Rathenau so celebrated by all republicans.

If we have recalled this paradigm of modern German statecraft it was only to confirm this so frightful example lying so close to us of a defenceless and weapon-less nation having to simply put up with everything, even every derision. Against this is valid for us the belief in an externally powerful state which alone can guarantee peace and

---

36 [Walther Rathenau (1867-1922) was a Jewish industrialist and politician who served as Minister of Reconstruction in 1921 and Foreign Minister in 1922. His insistence that Germany should fulfil its obligations under the Treaty of Versailles provoked the hostility of German nationalists and he was assassinated in June 1922. The Weimar government's reaction to this assassination was the promulgation in July 1922 of the Republikschutzgesetz (Law for the protection of the republic) which Feder often refers to.]

The German State on a National and Socialist Foundation

freedom. We dispense with historical reasons, this is not the task of a manifesto but a matter for the historian.

The counterpart of the idea of externally directed power politics is the internally directed rigid constitutional state. We came rather close to this ideal condition in the Bismarckian power state but in the fields that concerned the financial system and the unlimited recognition of private property and the demands that were derived therefrom our legal ideas stood fully under the capitalistic idea.

It requires no special emphasis that in terms of internal politics National Socialism stands unconditionally on the standpoint of the law insofar as everybody should be equal before the law and there should be no differences in social orders. But an essential transformation must be realised with respect to the basic idea of the law which signifies to the German an inner need, a voluntary subordination to the higher interests of the whole, whereas the prescriptions of the law valid among us today appear simply as a commandment of power and indeed as commandments of a power that does not stand in the service of the whole but, precisely in relation to the questions of property, has placed the protection of property before the protection of the person. The question of the new ordering of the public law will have to be discussed further in greater detail in another section.

Now we turn briefly to the questions of the external state form. A final decision on this question is in no way urgent. It can in general be solved only after a quite basic purging of our internal political conditions. The only possible way to this internal political purging seems to us to be exclusively through a dictatorship which with total determination cuts off and burns the sources of decomposition and disease in our national body.

The demands that we place on such a leader are extraordinarily high; a passionate love for his people, an unbending will, a virtual somnambulistic certainty in all his decisions must distinguish him. That his intellectual capacities must rise above the average is self-evident, but knowledge and capacities in the different fields are not the decisive factor. Knowledge and learning can be realised by others – How many men there are of high knowledge, great clarity of thought, of great intuition, the finest artistic talent – but if the last thing is lacking in them, the passionate will, the unswerving impulse, based on the deepest moral seriousness, then they will never stride forward at the head of nations, as trailblazers and leaders, to new heights.

I. The Foundations

We think of religious figures like Christ and Luther, Savonarola[37] and Mohammed, statesmen like Bismarck and Cromwell, generals like Friedrich the Great and Yorck,[38] etc. The dictator must be completely free of all unnecessary restrictions and hesitations, for him there cannot be any inevitabilities, for it must be he who makes history and he seizes with a daring determined hand when his his hour strikes, he embodies the longing of the nation, and therefore he never errs and is borne by the fanatic love of those to whom his deed brings liberation. He must be able to hate, so strongly and ruthlessly as he loves his people and his sacred task. In relation to his assistants and colleagues he stands as the first among free and equal people.

This old German idea forms the foundation of this iron connection between the leader and his friends for the sake of the cause. He is the leader because he has proved himself, and so long as he proves himself.

> Every power seems as it were redoubled by his presence
> He draws forth every latent energy,
> Showing to each his own peculiar talent,
> Yet leaving all to be what nature made them,
> And watching only that they be naught else
> In the right place and time.
>   (Schiller, Wallenstein)[39]

He is strict and hard with regard to himself, he orients himself according to his own laws. He has time for and listens to everybody, but he is quite able to differentiate between the important and the unimportant.

For the accomplishment of his goal he may not be afraid of blood and war, he may not rest and relax until his goal is reached, then he secures his creation further as far as this is humanly possible, but he

---

37 [Girolamo Savonarola (1452-1498) was a Dominican friar who preached against the corruption of the state and clergy and prophesied that Florence would become a powerful New Jerusalem if it corrected its moral vices. His additional refusal to support Pope Alexander VI's Holy League against France provoked his excommunication in 1497 and execution the following year.]

38 [Ludwig Graf Yorck von Wartenburg (1759-1830) was a Prussian Field Marshal who opposed the Prussian General Julius von Grawert's cooperation with the French during Napoleon's invasion of Russia in 1812 and was thus instrumental in the formation of the Sixth Coalition against Napoleon that ended in Napoleon's exile to Elba in 1814.]

39 [Friedrich Schiller, *Die Piccolomini*, the first play in his Wallenstein trilogy (1799). The translation is that of Samuel Taylor Coleridge].

The German State on a National and Socialist Foundation

can himself withdraw, as the dictator Sulla did, and thereby secures his work in a twofold manner in that he operates from a distance but still does not force everything through his strong personality to be measured by extraordinary standards; on the other hand, a freer and more independent following will be able to develop if the Titan does not constantly determine the political daily life but remains the leader in the spiritual sense. Such a brilliance of action and will will distinguish the dictator who will again lead Germany to new heights. If then the way out of the mire is found through the accomplishment of an extraordinary leader, the internal and external preconditions for an independent national life will have been regained, then the nation may once again decide regarding the external form of the state.

Our view of the future state form will be essentially influenced by the manner in which certain forms of the public life, especially the suffrage and the popular representation deriving therefrom, will be constituted. We could certainly think of the possibility of a healthy republican state form, rather as in ancient Rome. Indeed, almost all historical memories in Germany point to the monarchical state form. Now, with the monarchical state form is in no way inseparably bound the dynastic idea. On the contrary, it seems that only too often dynastic interests have developed greatly to the harm of nations.

Another factor admonishes us to extreme caution in the question of a possible reintroduction of the monarchic state form – the consequence of heritability among dynasties. In the painful history of the German people one may find repeatedly that the third generation after a significant ruler has squandered the heritage of its forefathers, damaged the honour and worthiness of the nation, lost the position of power of the empire, and destroyed the peace and welfare of the citizens. What the German imagines when he speaks of the advantages of the monarchy especially under a hereditary ruling house is always the thought of those to whom history has given the epithet "the Great".

We think thereby of Charles the Great,[40] Otto the Great,[41] Frederick the Great and the few who are ranked on a par with these real rulers;

---

40 [Charlemagne (ca.742-814) became King of the Franks in 768 and extended his rule beyond Francia into a Carolingian empire that included most of western Europe.]

41 [Otto the Great (912-973) was the Duke of Saxony who became king of the Germans in 936, defeated the Magyars in 955 and conquered the kingdom of Italy in 961. In 962 he was crowned emperor by Pope John XII and reigned from Rome as the Holy Roman Emperor.]

I. The Foundations

but just a fleeting memory of the gallery of incapacity, indolence, selfishness, prodigality, fantasy, distance from the people, and other dangerous characteristics that are bound with the names of Louis the Pious,[42] Otto III,[43] Wenceslaus,[44] Charles VI,[45] Friedrich Wilhelm III,[46] Wilhelm II[47] suffices to recognise clearly that the dynastic state form in no way includes a guarantee of the welfare of the nation.

That which expresses the inclination of the German to monarchy is the need of the German for a leader, and the readiness to subordinate himself to a leader. Precisely this last characteristic is perhaps an especially typical characteristic of the German, we know only too well this trait of the German character in its good and bad aspects. The loyalty unto death allowed him fight for and win the most powerful

---

42 [Louis le Pieux (778-840) was the son of Charlemagne, with whom he ruled as co-emperor from 813. In 817 he divided his empire among his three sons and his nephew Bernard, who ruled as King of Italy. However, Bernard rebelled against his uncle and was punished with a sentence of blinding, soon after which he died. Louis atoned for his cruelty publicly and thereby lost much of his prestige as a ruler. The Frankish empire was marked by civil wars during the remainder of his reign.]

43 [Otto III (980-1002) was the Holy Roman Empire from 996 and faced much opposition during his reign from the Slavic peoples so that he was forced to abandon the imperial territories east of the Elbe, though he nevertheless succeeded in consolidating the influence of Christianity in Poland and Hungary.]

44 [Václav I (ca.907-935) of the Přemyslid dynasty was Duke of Bohemia from 921. In 929, Bohemia was attacked by the east Frankish king, Henry the Fowler and forced to resume payment of tribute to the latter. Václav was murdered by a group of nobles in league with his brother Boleslav, who became the next Duke of Bohemia.]

45 [Charles VI (1368-1422) was called 'le bien-aimé '(the Beloved) as well as 'le fou' (the Mad). He suffered from bouts of madness and his reign was marked by the continuing conflicts of the so-called Hundred Years' War. Charles' ongoing feud with Burgundy was taken advantage of by Henry V of England, who defeated the French at the Battle of Agincourt in 1415. By the Treaty of Troyes signed in 1420, Henry was given Charles VI's daughter Catherine in marriage as well as the succession to the throne of France.]

46 [Friedrich Wilhelm III (1770-1840) was King of Prussia from 1797. Although he tried to pursue a policy of neutrality in the Napoleonic wars and did not join the Third Coalition, he was forced by the pro-war party which his queen Luise supported to join the Fourth Coalition of 1806 which led to the Battle of Jena in which Prussia was defeated by Napoleon.]

47 [Wilhelm II (1859-1941) was the last German emperor and reigned from 1888 to November 1918. Wilhelm did not support Bismarck's strict anti-Socialist laws and dismissed the chancellor in 1890. When Austria was forced to attack Serbia after the assassination of Archduke Franz Ferdinand in Sarajevo, he decided to support Austria-Hungary even though he was aware of the dangers of a war that might involve Russia, France and England.]

The German State on a National and Socialist Foundation

victories, it allowed him to follow even foreign flags; but it includes also very much lack of independence among the weaker types to the point of worthlessness and slavishness, love of things foreign and lack of judgement. The question regarding the succession is therefore, in Germany itself, not hard to solve. The much harder question lies in the problem of the leader.

The selection of the leader has up to now been more or less always left to pure chance. The princely marital bed is indeed in no way a guarantee of the intellectual capacity and of the necessary character traits that are by all means to be demanded of a monarch. And if we remember the modern German economy, where mere membership in the party decides on the qualification for the highest official posts, we must give this question special attention.

The difficulty lies, in any case, in the safeguarding of the moral and character qualities of the one in whose hands the destiny of the people should be laid. While however a dictator takes the leadership upon himself from himself, as the bearer of the national longing, a future leader must emerge actually from the conscious will of the nation as the best and most suited. Thereby it may remain completely open whether the highest worth should be united in one person or whether the state leadership should be constituted of two or more. In any case, one thing stands firm for us, that the one entrusted with the leadership of the highest state affairs, whether it be crowned heads or a consular duum- or triumvirate, the highest responsibility will, in the best possible case, be anchored in the constitution. Highest responsibility will therefore be the most essential national political foundation that will distinguish the National Socialist state from the previous forms of rule.

A special aspect of the national political foundations of the National Socialist state is the demand for a nationalist state in which the members of foreign countries and races are excluded from the leadership of the state affairs as well as from the assumption of public offices.

The great lesson of the whole of German history can be summarised in the fact that Germany was always poor, weak and miserable when its rulers pursued foreign interests and when the narrow small concerns of the individual provinces and cities were placed above the common affairs of the Reich; and likewise was Germany always strong and powerful when it was united and its rulers thought and felt in a German way and the provinces and cities felt as members of the great

I. The Foundations

common fatherland. Closing of the nation externally with all freedom and diversity internally. This is the correct idea of a German state. The Bismarck Reich already came very close to this ideal of the idea of the German state, only that our racial brothers in German Austria[48] still remained outside the Reich.

The unification of all German tribes in a closed national state is therefore our most distinguished national political goal. Internal politically the federative and federal character of the larger provinces as it was produced historically is to be maintained or rebuilt. The national political base lines in this respect are the following: All functions of the Reich in which it is a question of the power political position of the German Reich with regard to foreign countries are matters of the Reich. These are the Foreign Office, embassies and consulates, the passport system, the control of foreign trade, the customs system and, above all, the army and navy. Internal politically, on the other hand, the idea of the most far-reaching independence of the individual provinces or federal states is to be fostered. Financial independence is the precondition for the independent existence of the nation, so the tax legislation will have to be delegated mainly to the provinces.

The legislation for the civil, trade, and penal law will be regulated by the law of the Reich, but subordinated in practice to the provincial justice and police authorities. In a similar way the transport institutions will certainly be regulated according to directives of the law of the Reich but they will nevertheless remain, in their finances and administratively and operationally, under the provincial sovereignty.

That the freedom of religion should remain fully upheld by the constitution requires no special mention; on the other hand, religions whose writings are not written fully in the German language and accessible to everybody and whose content contain doctrines dangerous to the state will not enjoy this protection.

The constitutional form of the basic socialist character of the Reich is stressed especially in the field of labour law as well as in the fields of

---

48 [The Republic of German Austria was the name given to the state formed in 1918 after the first World War from the German-speaking lands of the Austro-Hungarian Empire. It included, apart from the current Austrian territories, South Tyrol and Tarvisio (now in Italy), southern Carinthia and southern Styria (now in Slovenia) and the Sudetenland and German Bohemia (now in the Czech Republic).]

illness, accident, old age and disability insurance and will be better implemented than happens today.

Insights and Goal-Setting

If every thorough treatment of matters related to time demands an answer to the three questions: How is it now? How did it come about? and What now? - for without this basic investigation a complete and conscientious work is never to be expected – this is valid in a higher sense when it is a matter of building a new state. A description of the present-day situation within the scope of this work naturally has a place only insofar as it is a question of extracting the essential characteristics of the present-day critical conditions of the state and economy. In such a task one must especially avoid taking any symptoms as causes. This is precisely the art of every diagnosis that is not deceived by externalities or excrescences but looks deeper into the reason of things. This becomes most clear in the medical example or in the case of a living man. If a swelling appears somewhere in the body the cause is to be sought first in the ailment of the concerned part of the body; the fact that this part of the body is diseased has its cause in a bad condition of the blood; but even this knowledge is not to be considered as the last cause but the bad condition of the blood will in turn be the consequence of bad or insufficient nourishment. Now, the cure would not be able to succeed if the doctor combated only the external phenomenon; thereby a temporary alleviation would in the best case set in, a soothing of the pains, but the illness would continue. Even an attempt at a cure through a blood-purifying treatment would not be able to bring a lasting cure if the basic cause, namely the deficient or bad nourishment or the other harmful circumstances, were not removed. Only such a treatment from within outwards can bring a real cure. This is clear to everybody. Precisely so must the investigation be undertaken if we have to do with a sick national body. Even here it is very little useful if the external symptoms of the illness are combated. One feels only too well as a sad truth the well-known saying: "The small rogues are hanged, the big ones are allowed to go free". The frequency of violations against the common interest is only the external sign of the fact that behind the scenes things are played out that harm the common welfare to a great degree. For, only if something is rotten in the state can such great damages persist and become a lasting danger for the existence of the state itself. If thus the state itself is sick, it is to be supposed with the greatest probability that the cause thereof is wrong intellectual attitudes with regard to popular concerns and with regard to the actual functions and authority of the state itself.

I. The Foundations

A cure can therefore be expected, in the final analysis, from a new healthy idea of the state, through the creation of a healthy powerful state leadership which is fully independent and not burdened with the sins of the past. Every solution that takes its point of departure from a compromise with the existing powers or that seeks to bind itself again to the collapsed forms of the earlier state bears the seed of its own decay in itself. In this connection one must also be warned against binding oneself to historical state forms that were indeed not bad in themselves but still very quickly succumbed to a collapse.

What now are the most striking characteristics of the present-day crisis?

Externally and superficially – as in the case of a fever – high temperature or, translated into economic political terms: agitation, tenseness on every occasion, unrest and disorder. It is extremely significant that every stuffy and lazy person, but also the entire army of the actual debtors, have always praised with the loudest voice "rest and order" as the cure-all. Rest and order is naturally not a political goal in general but only a condition that shows that healthy conditions rule within the national body. But if a nation is sick, it is quite natural and self-evident that this manifests itself in unrest and disorder. A political attitude that preaches and seeks to establish only "rest and order" is therefore fully wrongly oriented; on the other hand, it only helps the illness to enter ever deeper, until death enters with the most frightful cramps. Even ulcers and suppurations, thought of as personified, naturally wish likewise that the sick person would remain pretty quiet for the bacilli can then multiply so wonderfully quickly and spread over the entire body and fully putrefy it also internally. No, quite on the contrary: away with the suppurations! These must be cut out, one cannot adduce the pains of the operative attack as a counter-reason; the patient must be brought out of his bad environment, and above all he must receive a healthy and strong diet.

The further symptoms are the filling of state positions with unsuitable elements, the disposal of state matters through majority decisions, the occurrence of such majority decisions in the parliament as do not bear any responsibility, the election of such parliaments according to a suffrage which externally is indeed the most free and universal but internally speculates on the lack of judgement of the masses and simply suppresses better insight and higher feeling of responsibility. A government that is dependent on parliamentary majorities - which come about purely by chance and for which only the party political considerations are decisive - can naturally for its part no longer be the objective guardian of the common welfare but it is the stamping ground for ambitious party politicians and obstinate doctrinaires. All these symptoms may be summed up in the word "parliamentarianism".

This parliamentarianism is the great democratic lie of the capacity of the people for self-government. Of course we may think that responsibility-conscious state citizens are completely capable of judging in an authoritative way on public matters and of leading the fate of their community or country, but a suffrage like the universal one, direct and secret for persons above 21 years of both sexes, bears in itself necessarily the seed of the vile rule of the inferior and unscrupulous.

Along with the vile rule of the parliaments and the governments depending thereupon, there rules today in reality, in spite of all the anti-capitalistic slogans of the Marxists, large loan capital. High finance is the unrestricted ruler of the state and economy. No government dares to take any drastic measures against the profit interests of the banking and stock-exchange world. All the nations have become bound in interest and toll to this supra-national world power through quite gigantic national debts. The results of this interest slavery are enormous, they shake the entire world to its foundations in economic and national political relations. Interest collection has indeed become the major work of the governments. This means for the nations a frightful tax exploitation and draining through the diverse methods of direct and, especially, indirect taxes, through an unstoppably progressive inflation which has led at its peak to a robbing of the entire middle-class of their savings. This unrestricted rule of the money-bag exercises, behind the mask of the legal claim to interest, the most brutal rule that has ever governed the world. It leads to an impoverishment and pauperisation of the masses and especially of those circles to whom the acquisition of money is not a goal in itself and therefore not the central point of their entire thought. Only from this arises the most frightful consequence of this absolute financial rule, that is, the moral degradation of the peoples standing under this rule. All instincts are directed to acquisition and possession, all concepts of loyalty and faith sink in the ruthless pursuit of gain, the respectable man is forced to experience that, as reward for his respectability, he must sink ever deeper down while unscrupulousness brings gigantic profits in the case of all possible and impossible businesses. Desperately large circles struggle for their livelihood, a bearable income through work alone becomes increasingly more difficult.

I. The Foundations

In closed frontlines the workers seek to extort ever higher wages, strikes shake the economic work places, lame their production and indirectly harm therewith most of all those who are dependent on the greatest possible production of goods for the national economy, precisely the workers themselves.

As a total phenomenon we can summarise these conditions under the concept of "Mammonism".

The reverse side of this Mammonism is the Marxist world-view born of the intellectual mood of the victims of the Mammonistic violation. We know very well that the masterminds of the Marxists have cleverly been able to use this intellectual mood for themselves as handlers for international capital and, at the same time, to divert from themselves the hatred of the exploited, but we have to deal here with an intellectual disposition that stands not only in an obstructive but in a most highly hostile way against the re-establishment of a healthy national state.

The essence of Marxism we must glimpse in the fact that it denies private property and therewith cuts the ground from every economy and, beyond that, every higher culture; further, in the fact that it has fostered the idea of class-struggle and therewith torn the people apart into different classes mutually fighting one another. It is enough to point to the nameless misery of the Russian people, where, in the Soviet state, this erroneous nation- and economy-killing doctrine was translated into reality in the highest measure.

And if we now look for the actual pathogens of the disease, we strangely come up everywhere against Jews as leaders and chief beneficiaries.

The Jewish question is becoming a world-question on whose solution the welfare and woe of the nations will be dependent.

To this question a special work will be devoted in this Library series.[49]

A review of history shows us that the desperate nations have over and over again sought to liberate themselves from this evil through bloody suppression and eradication of individual Jews – but after some generations the Jews have returned once again stronger and financially more powerful after such pogroms.

---

49 [Feder's work on the Jews, *Die Juden*, was published in 1933 as vol.45 of the Nationalsozialistische Bibliothek]

The German State on a National and Socialist Foundation

We must therefore avoid looking for the solution of the Jewish question in this primitive manner – indeed one cannot kill the plague bacillus individually, one can only eradicate it by cutting off its life necessities from it.

The anti-Semitism flaring up in the whole world is the torch-signal that the nations have recognised their greatest and most deadly enemy, but it is now our task to direct this correct emotive knowledge in a correct, reasonable way.

The battle against Marxism and therewith against the Jews succeeds through untiring education of the poisoned masses. It is the first stage of our battle.

The breaking of the interest slavery is the last and hardest battle in the economic field for the liberation of the people and state from the golden network of the supra-national financial power.

Only after fighting through these stages, and when the victory has been fully wrested and secured, would it be time to carry out all the further reforms that will give the debilitated and sick national body a new will to live and new vital force that will first realise what is in all our minds, in which we all believe with glowing hearts and which we strive for with unbending will:

Germany's rebirth.

A new, free, united Greater Germany in a healthy, firm and powerful state of work and performance.

II. The Programme

The Origin of the Programme

Every work requires a plan, every realisation must be preceded by intellectual creation. The more clearly and better worked out the construction plans are the more beautifully and quickly the building will be erected. Even new political structures requires a clear construction plan, this is called here a political programme.

The demands that must be placed on a political programme are very high and very diverse. It is a question of a task of the highest responsibility, for the welfare and woe of one's own people depends on whether the plan was good. A programme must further deal, with the most concise brevity, with all the important fields of public life, must withstand every criticism, may not lose itself in details, may not offer the opponents any unnecessary weak points, may not awaken any Utopian hopes that cannot later be satisfied. The programme must be a faithful image of the coming state and the new economy. It must show everybody in outlines the sketch of the state- and economic order that is desired, but it may not also constrain or anticipate the execution in its details.

Every programme also has a history and a development, but it is certainly a touchstone of the fundamental correctness of a movement if, after so many years, nothing essential must be changed in its basic features and only some obscurities must be removed. Only the most important and striking programme point of the old programme of 24 February 1923, no.11, "Abolition of income without work and effort, breaking of the interest slavery" urgently requires a thorough programmatic treatment in national-, financial- and economic political terms. The detailed treatment of this point was at that time not such an absolute necessity because, at that time, the more detailed writings related to this, Manifesto for the breaking of the interest slavery and The state bankruptcy, its solution, were almost the only existing writings and were fully known and familiar to the founders

II. The Programme

and first followers of the movement. In a way it was the intellectual content of these writings that added the socialist scope of activity - with plans that had already at that time been determined in their fundamental features - to the will to renewal that had brought together a small circle around Anton Drexler[50] and Adolf Hitler, to the circle of nationalist and populist ideas.

It is precisely these programme points and demands through which the German freedom movement of National Socialism essentially and fundamentally differentiates itself from all other populist and nationalist groups, movements and parties, and through which it differentiates itself especially from all so-called parliamentary parties which are, for their part, only a manifestation of the Mammonistic-plutocratic rule.

A further necessity in the new formulation of the programme was to obtain a clearer form and a clear structuring regarding the individual fields of public life. This has happened.

It is my duty here to think of yet another ground-breaking work which owes its origin to a parallel manifestation of National Socialism in Austria and Bohemia, I mean the book (published in Troppau) of the engineer Jung,[51] representative for the Sudeten Germans in Czechoslovakia in the Prague Parliament.

Austrian National Socialism in its beginnings goes far back to the time before the war. Its scope of ideas rested more on the attempt to bring the socialist world of ideas into harmony with the nationalist idea, whereas the German National Socialism of the Reich that arose only after the collapse – indeed without knowledge of the existence of this Austrian National Socialism - adopted from the start a fundamental battle stance against Marxism.

Today the two movements have come together in their common goals.

---

50 [Anton Drexler (1884-1942) was, along with Dietrich Eckart and Feder, one of the founders of the German counterpart of the originally Austrian Deutsche Arbeiter Partei in Munich. Drexler served as honorary president of the party, of which Hitler had already in 1921 become the clear leader. Drexler left the party in 1923 and rejoined when Hitler rose to power in 1933.]

51 [See above p.8.]

The National And Economic Programme of the National Socialist German Workers' Party

Our goal is – Germany's rebirth in a German spirit to a German freedom.

The way to this main goal is:

I. The national political principle: The German Reich is the home of the Germans.

a) In Foreign Policy:

1. The establishment of a closed national state that includes all Germans.

2. The powerful representation of German interests abroad.

b) In Racial Policy:

3. The removal of the Jews and all non-Germans from all responsible positions in public life.

4. Prohibition of immigration of eastern Jews and other parasitical foreigners. Troublesome foreigners and Jews may be deported.

c) In Civic Policy:

5. Only the German who pledges himself to the German culture and community can exercise state citizenship rights.

6. One who is not a German can live only as a guest in the German state and stands under foreign law.

7. The rights and interests of the Germans go before those of the members of foreign nations.

II. The economic political principle: The task of the national economy is the fulfilment of demand and not as high a profitability as possible for loan capital.

8. National Socialism fundamentally recognises private property and places it under state protection.

II. The Programme

9. The welfare of the people however draws a limit to the immoderate hoarding of wealth in the hands of individuals.

10. All Germans form a work community for the promotion of the common welfare and culture.

11. Within the scope of this general work obligation of every German and with fundamental acknowledgement of private property is allowed to every German a free possibility of acquisition and free disposal of his work income.

12. The healthy combination of small-, medium- and big businesses in all fields of the economic life, thus also in agriculture, remains upheld.

13. Gigantic enterprises (corporations, syndicates and trusts) will be combated.

14. Usury and racketeering, as well as ruthless enrichment at the cost and harm of the people, will be punished with death.

15. The introduction of a year of compulsory work for every German.

III. The financial political principle: The financial system stands in the service of the state, the financial powers may not form a state within the state; thus our goal: Breaking of the interest slavery through:

16. Liberation of the state and therewith the people from its interest-bound debt to large loan capital.

17. Nationalisation of the Reichsbank Pub.Ltd.Co., and the central banks.

18. The financing of all large public tasks (development of hydro-energy, roadways, etc.) with avoidance of loans through the issuance of interest-free state treasury vouchers or through a cash-free method.

19. The introduction of a stable currency on a covered basis.

20. The creation of a non-profit Construction and Economic Bank (currency reform) for the granting of interest-free credit.

21. Thorough restructuring of the tax system according to socialist, national economic principles. Liberation of consumption from the burden of indirect taxes and production from constricting taxes (tax reform and tax exemption).

IV. The social political principle: The common welfare is the highest law.

22. Generous development of old age insurance through nationalisation of the life-annuity system. To every needy German national comrade an adequate pension will be guaranteed from a certain age or in the case of a premature occurrence of permanent inability to earn a living.

23. The sharing of all people engaged in productive enterprises according to performance and age in the revenues of the work with an accompanying share in the responsibility for the fulfilment of the national economic tasks of the work.

24. The confiscation of all war- and revolution-profits not based on honest work as well as of property acquired through hoarding and usury and their use for the development of social insurance.

25. Removal of the housing shortage through comprehensive new housing buildings throughout the Reich by means of the new non-profit Construction and Economic Bank to be created according to Art.21.

V. Cultural-politically: A blossoming of all the sciences and fine arts on the foundation of a politically free, economically healthy state is our chief cultural goal.

This should be reached through

26. The education of the youth into physically healthy and intellectually free men according to the great traditions of German intellectual life.

27. Full freedom of religion and conscience.

28. Special protection of the Christian faith.

29. Suppression and exclusion of religious doctrines that go against

the German moral feeling and whose content bear a state- and nation-destroying character.

30. Suppression of all harmful influences in literature and the press, stage, art and cinema.

31. Freedom of instruction in the German universities, formation of a ruling class of men of character.

VI. Militarily:

32. Making the nation defensible through the introduction of military law for every free German.

33. Abolition of mercenary troops.

34. The creation of a militia army for the defence of the homeland under a professional officer corps to be built up through a strict hierarchical discipline.

VII. Other reforms:

35. Reform of the press system. Suppression of all press instruments that contravene the concerns of the German people. The strictest responsibility for all news that is falsely or tendentiously distorted.

36. Reform of the suffrage with the abolition of the current corrupting forms of election campaign and the lack of responsibility of the elected (immunity).

37. Development of professional chambers.

38. Reform of the judiciary in the field of Land law – (fundamental recognition of the right to property in land, non-leasability of land on the part of private capital, preemption right of the state, and reversion of land to the state in case of careless management).

    Civil law – (far stricter protection of personal honour and of health, as against the one-sided legal protection of property ruling today).

39. Constitutional reforms:

The German State on a National and Socialist Foundation

Constitution. The constitution corresponding to the German character is a sovereign state leadership focussed in a highest position. - Whether this highest position is occupied by a monarch to be elected by the people or by two or three responsible highest Reich officials must be left for later determination by the people.

Federal character of the Reich. The composition of the German people from different provinces internally bound through tribes and history conditions the comprehensive independence of the individual federal states with respect to their internal affairs.

The concern of the Reich is the representation of the German people externally, passports and tolls, and, further, the army and navy.

Three principal opponents stand in the way of the accomplishment of this national- and economic programme of National Socialism. Marxism, parliamentarianism and, ranged above both, large loan capital.

1. Our anti-Marxist battle is directed against the state-disintegrating doctrine of the Jew Karl Marx, against the people-disintegrating doctrine of class-struggle, against the economy-disintegrating doctrine of the denial of private property and against the purely economic materialistic conception of history.

2. Our anti-parliamentarian battle is directed against the irresponsibility of the so-called popular representatives who – immune – never actually have to take responsibility for the consequences of their decisions, as well as against all damages produced therefrom (corruption, nepotism, bribability) and, as the worst consequence - a government dependent on such a parliament.

3. Our anti-Mammonistic battle, which is ranged above the other two battle-fronts, is directed against the world-encompassing financial power, that is, against the permanent financial and economic bleeding and exploitation of our people through large loan capital.

This battle however is, on the other hand, also a powerful intellectual struggle against the soul-destroying materialistic spirit of egoism and avarice with all its concomitant corrupting manifestations in all fields of our public, economic and cultural life.

II. The Programme

In the last and deepest analysis, it is a matter of the battle of two world-views that are expressed through two fundamentally different intellectual structures – the productive and creative spirit and the mobile avaricious spirit. The creative spirit rooted in the soil and yet again overcoming the world in metaphysical experience finds its principal representatives in Aryan man – the avaricious, rootless commercial and materialistic spirit directed purely to the this-worldly finds its principal representative in the Jew.

National Socialism like Anti-Semitism glimpses in the Jewish-materialistic spirit the primary root of the evil, but it also knows that this most powerful battle of world-history cannot remain standing in purely negative anti-Semitic demands, therefore the entire national- and economic programme of National Socialism rises far above the certainly ground-breaking but negative anti-Semitic battle by positively giving a creative constructive image of how the National Socialist state of work and performance should look.

If this main goal is reached, then the National Socialist Party will be dissolved. National Socialism will then have become the life-content of the entire German people. The National Socialist German Workers' Party is indeed in general not a parliamentary party in the customary sense of the word, but only the determined, forward-looking and future-oriented section of the population that has gathered together around a leader strong in will and mind, in order to lead Germany out of shame and powerlessness externally, out of destruction and corruption internally, to a powerful and imposing position externally, and, internally, to an economically sound, culturally blooming, intellectually and morally high-standing national community.

We wish to build the Reich of German longing as Geibel[52] sings it:

> One externally, with a mighty sword,
> Rallying round a high banner,
> Internally rich and manifold,
> Every tribe in its own way!

---

52 [Emanuel Geibel (1815-1884) was a German poet and dramatist who wrote several patriotic poems that were attacked by the contemporary liberal 'Young German' literary circle around the Jewish writers, Heinrich Heine and Ludwig Börne, but later championed by the National Socialists].

III. The State

Structure of the National Socialist state

The National Socialist idea of the German State

Already in the chapter on the power political foundations we have pointed to the fact that every deviation of the German rulers from their purely German tasks was accompanied by the most baneful consequences for the German people. If one surveys German history one always finds the German longing for a closed national state realised only in short historical periods, over and over again this German dream faded away, and over and over again Germany sank back in powerlessness and disintegration. Thereby there stands firm from the entire German history one lesson that only the closing of the nation within a powerfully led state enables Germany to resist the enormous dangers which arise to it merely from its unfavourable geopolitical situation. Almost nowhere does Germany have natural boundaries, almost everywhere it lies free and unprotected against hostile inroads. Neither the sea that girdles England nor the high mountains which separate Spain and Italy from its neighbours give Germany a natural defence. France has only one open side against us, Russia the same. Only Germany lies in the middle between the other nations – as the heart – and as the battlefield of Europe. On German soil battled Spanish, French, English, Swedish, Russian and Mongol armies, on German soil were the frightful religious wars of the Thirty Years' War fought, and conversely Germans bled in foreign service for foreign interests in all the lands. Mother Germania bled from thousands of wounds that were struck by its foreign armies and – that were struck in her by the strife of her own sons. Endlessly tragic is German history, so tragic that the German longing for a unified, closed German Reich was included in fairy-tales, in the sagas of old Barbarossa in the Kyffhäuser.[53] Through centuries the realisation of the German state idea remained – a longing and hope of the best

---

53 [The Kyffhäuser range of hills between the states of Thuringia and Saxony-Anhalt is considered to be the resting place of the Holy Roman Emperor, Friedrich Barbarossa (1122-1190), who drowned in the Saleph river in Turkey during the Third Crusade.]

III. The State

people of the nation, until, in 1871, a mighty smith forged the Germany unity. Much remained to be desired in the realisation of the Great German state that was to include all Germans who live in territorial connection with the motherland. But already this partial realisation of the German longing granted us a high flowering of German history as seldom before.

But we do not have to reckon with 'ifs' and 'buts', rather, we have to learn from history. Politics is history that is becoming, and if from the "making of history" salvation should bloom for our people then our statecraft, our national politics must, with respect for that which has come about in history, avoid the mistakes of earlier times and bind themselves to the best tradition. The man, the politician without a history who dogmatically makes history from his armchair, will be able to bring only calamity on a people as we have experienced it in the last years from the new German Marxist government-showmen. As disastrous and pernicious is the complete breakdown of the old social form, especially when this destruction is identical to the force of the Marxist movement, so little may the old be preserved merely because it is old. Herein lies once again the tragedy of the conservative spirit, that, creatively unfruitful and without imagination, it rejects everything new just because it is new, and because it holds fast tenaciously to outdated forms which have lost their substance a long time ago. People and state are not mummies and constructions, but living entities; the clothes cut once do not suit forever. Only some quite large basic traits are drawn through the destiny of nations, and a neglect of such basic knowledge has always avenged itself bitterly on the nations. For us Germans the fundamental historical national political doctrine is: "Be unified!"

The word "united"[54] however does not mean "unity"[55] but "being in agreement".[56] Only from the agreement of the German tribes on the principles of external and internal politics can there grow as its finest flower an internally free state that is externally powerful with international weight.

For the German state therefore there may not be any European or international economic, church or humanitarian motives but only exclusively the welfare of the entire German nation. I mean "motives"

---

54 ["einig"]
55 ["Einheit"]
56 ["Einigkeit"]

for political action. Alongside there run naturally the influences of a church-, economic- and generally human character which must be adequately valued and considered. But the principle must be and remain that the German national state has to represent only Germans and this in internal politics as well as in external.

Our national political goal therefore is:

1. The establishment of a closed national state which includes all Germans.

2. The powerful representation of all German interests abroad.

The Nationalist Idea

The precondition for the awakening or, better, for the reawakening of a strong national consciousness is the removal of all Jews and non-Germans from all responsible positions in public life.

The determined defensive battle against the invasion of the Jews in almost all fields of our public life is carried out with total energy only by National Socialism. The battle against Jewry is the conscious struggle for the German spirit and for German freedom.

The influence and effect of the Jews on their host peoples cannot at all be compared with the power relations and the battles of other peoples but only with the struggle for life and death between a healthy body and the deadly poisonous germs that have attacked it. When a living organism is attacked by poisonous bacilli the question is only: either the healthy force of the body will become master of the foreign intruders – then it cuts them out – or it will no longer be master of them, then it will die on account of them. So also for the host peoples of the Jews everywhere in the world there is only this: either cut the Jews out of the national body – or die on account of the Jew.

Precisely the comparison with the human body and the germs shows us very graphically how lopsided the favourite misleading opinion is, that the Jews worked their way up everywhere only on account of their greater efficiency and it is highly wrong and unjust to attack and persecute them for that reason. One cannot simply say that the cholera bacillus is likewise so much stronger and efficient than the man and that is why it has overcome the healthy man – no, it is a poison for the man. And, precisely as in this battle of the living organism against invading

III. The State

poisons, special symptoms of poisoning appear accompanied by fever conditions, cramps, symptoms of paralysis, etc., so the battle of the nations attacked by the Jew is expressed in quite similar symptoms of disease – unrest and agitation in the civic and political life, powerful convulsions in the national body, turmoil, terror, civil war alternating with quite typical paralysis symptoms especially in the intellectual parts of the nations – in the governments. Then there is only one question, whether the nationally conscious circles recognising the enemy succeed in warning and enlightening the governments or in forming the government and neutralising the Jews themselves – then the cure enters with certainty; if it does not succeed in doing this, then national death enters equally certainly. There is no third way. A temporary isolation – to remain with the medical imagery – brings about only apparent remedies: sooner or later the bacilli break out anew into the blood vessels of the body, the end of this second struggle is then deadly for the patient.

Decisive for the final success – as in life in general – is the will to power. Without this will to power – without this will to the maintenance of the nation the nation is helplessly delivered to a downfall. What does not literally go down becomes a slave, fellaheen, bondman and servant of the all-Jewish world-power.

It is a life and death battle. Many efficient soldiers have set out – but the majority of our national comrades are still asleep. Education over and over again, tireless, is the solution. What makes this education so especially difficult is the artlessness and softness of the Aryan precisely in these vital racial questions.

The strong racial mixture within our German people itself has doubtless almost completely buried the clear and high racial consciousness in too many so that only an indefinite feeling of aversion against the racially foreign Jews has remained instead of a a precise knowledge of racial laws. The Jew for his part has most strictly followed his racial laws for more than two thousand years in the clear knowledge of the outstanding importance of the maintenance of the purity of the blood for character and nation.[57]

On the other hand, he has been able to represent the racial agitation as outdated rubbish, which, with regard to the racial mixture in Germany, was unfortunately possible for him with a certain

---

57   Cf. the National Socialist Library volumes on race and the Jews!

The German State on a National and Socialist Foundation

appearance of justification. Instead of the the Jewish contempt for racial science on the part of the Germans being opposed with complete determination, by the demand: "German, keep your blood pure!", the German was inferior even in this field to the psychagogic arts[58] of the Jew. The century of the Enlightenment with its humanitarian ideals indeed brought to the Jews emancipation from the chains which had been forged by our forefathers in their higher wisdom against the infestation of the Jewish spirit of robbery and usury, but to ourselves only confusion and uncertainty on this fundamental question. With the sentence: "the Jews are also men" - a sentence which was and is indeed never disputed by anybody – the entry of the Jews to civic equal rights was granted. The national-racial resistance against the Jewish foreign folk of an entirely different intellectual structure was therewith lulled and the battle against the civic emancipation was therewith crippled from the start.

From this platform now there took place the conquest of our entire economic and, recently, public life up to the present situation of the unrestricted rule of the Jews.

An entire series of testimonies of the Jews themselves reveals that they feel as a state within a state, that they feel more closely bound to their racial comrades in other countries than to their host peoples.

From this Jewish feeling of belonging closely together among peoples are directly produced dangers for the indigenous peoples in the field of the foreign political relations of nations in war and peace.

At first, however, the attention of the Jews was directed to the demand for economic advantages. Here once again their unrestricted pursuit of profit, impaired by no social feelings for their host peoples, stood them in good stead.

As the inventors and bearers of the modern credit system it was soon an easy matter for them to bring the entire financial economy of the states and, through bank and stock-exchange, also of the private sector for the most part under their influence.

From here, thus after the creation of their financial position, Jewry stretched its fingers also to the intellectual-cultural products of the nation; here their moving spirit, their quick wit, their critical

---

58   [arts of persuasion]

III. The State

understanding - characteristics that may often appear as definite advantages to the serious, heavy, down-to-earth Aryan spirit - came to their help.

But in reality it was only the thieving instinct, their lack of conscience and unscrupulousness - which is already announced in their religious doctrines. For the Jew, according to the doctrines of the Schulchan Aruch,[59] the property of the non-Jew is like property without a master – there so that the Jew may appropriate it! The Jew set all the means of the banking and stock-exchange technique at his service. Anonymisation – the depersonalisation of our economy through the stock-marketable form of the public limited company – has to a certain degree separated capital from work, the share-holder knows in the rarest instances something of his factory, he has only the one-sided interest in the profitability of his money when he has invested it in the form of shares. This phenomenon has to be mentioned in this place because with this depersonalisation of our economy there goes hand in hand also its degradation. The entrepreneur and manufacturer who has built up his enterprise from scratch, who knows the requirements of his customers, who still has the old business honourableness and considers it as his duty to produce a solid, good, lasting product corresponding to the actual needs of the economy, this really solid entrepreneur is something so fundamentally different from the modern large share-holder who, with the purely capitalistic possession of a large share package knows only one interest, to aim at as high a return as possible. Whether in the enterprises good and cheap objects are manufactured, whether in general productive values are created by a stock company or, as in the case of the credit companies (banks) in general, no values are created is a matter of utmost indifference to the capitalist – the share-holder. This has as its further consequence that the production is oriented less to the needs, that, much rather, only an apparent need needs to be stirred up through enormous advertising. Earlier it was entirely forbidden in the code of honour of the entrepreneurs to extol one's products; one who did this was a market- crier, and such a market-crier-like extolling of one's wares was considered by the solid businessman to be dishonest competition. The Jewish trader however conducted precisely this sort of market-crying trade businesses with total insistence, wherein his arts of persuasion came in handy. Today in place of the importunate Jewish crier has appeared Jewish advertising.

---

59 [The Schulchan Aruch is the most authoritative code of Jewish law and was composed in 1563 in northern Israel by Yosef Karo.]

The German State on a National and Socialist Foundation

In the field of science there occurred a similar development, especially in the field of economic science – the so-called national economics. Gradually the task of national economics was seen no longer to lie in the investigation of the national economic legitimacies and necessities and in the derivation of guidelines for the economic leadership from the results of the investigations but increasingly only a description of the situation was carried out without investigating whether the economic phenomena and forms encountered were also good and suitable and applicable to the actual needs of the national economy. In this way people succeeded, and succeed today more than ever, in effecting the frightful damages to the economy and, therewith, to the national community – considered scientifically – and, for this reason, in an unchangeable manner. Into this field there enters especially the doctrine of the state and private credit services industry, and especially the doctrine of interest. We have dealt with this question in detail in another place, here it may suffice to point to the fact that basically that which we call national economy today is only a private capitalistic instruction to personal enrichment and a well arranged attempt at the justification of the usurious capitalistic robbery of the workforce of productive nations.

It is worth noting that among the lecturers of national economics there is a very large percentage of Jews.

To the layman more striking is the incursion of the Jews into the literary and artistic field.

One who considers our present-day theatre will be shocked at the baseness and cynicism that spreads there. Especially valid is this of the modern phenomenon of the cinema. The drama of lechers and rakes rules our stages; with subversive and clever dialectic, the good German is lectured that morality and ethics, honour and conscientiousness are basically sheer stupidity without which one can go farther. These attacks on the public are accompanied by the Jewish theatre-agency nuisance in which the knowledge of the artistically inclined tends to decide less than the gratitude to the theatre- and concert-agents of those seeking a position.

But then there followed on a wide scope the manipulation of public opinion through the daily press. Almost all the large newspapers gradually passed over to Jewish ownership. Therewith the circle around the German people was closed. To the economic rule was added the intellectual rule. Everything that was detrimental to the Jewish

III. The State

interests was withheld and silenced as long as possible from the public; if ideas or performances nevertheless asserted themselves, then began the real witch-hunt, at first through the attempt to make such efforts ridiculous, and, if even that did not help, lies and misrepresentation as well as personal denigration had to operate. Briberies, threats were attempted and finally one did not shy away even from economically ruining the inconvenient opponent or admonisher, or from even killing him.

This last most frightful weapon was generally not used, or only seldom, against private persons, for hardly ever did the reaction of a real friend of the people without a political or state position of power achieve a degree of effectiveness before he was already broken by the barrage of lies and calumny in the public organs of the Jews.

In the parties, the dissatisfaction of the masses was stoked through extreme exaggeration, and the class hatred against the propertied and their supposed protectors, the state authority and the army, was kindled. Even here – as everywhere in the case of these assaults on the national state - it was Jews who mostly agitated and fomented. It need only be recalled that Karl Marx, the founder of the Marxist doctrine of class-struggle, was indeed a Jew (Mardochai was his real name). His herald in Germany, Ferdinand Lassalle,[60] originally Feist Lasal, was likewise a Jew.

In the war and revolution then the Jewish work of destruction against the German state was completed. The princes were driven away, the epaulettes torn from the officers, the officials made compliant through hunger so that they may make their manpower - indispensable even to the socialist-high-capitalist state of modern Germany – available. In this way was the German nation disarmed, emasculated, robbed of its leaders, dispossessed and violated, demoralised and debilitated, while everywhere throughout public life, in economics and politics, in art and theatre, the Jews arrogated to themselves an unquestionable hegemony.

The foundation of their rule is their enormous wealth.

---

60   [Ferdinand Lassalle (1825-1864) was a German-Jewish socialist who was acquainted with Marx, though the latter considered him an opportunist on account of his willingness to compromise with the conservative Bismarck. Marx therefore did not support Lassalle when the latter founded an Allgemeiner Deutscher Arbeiterverein (General German Workers' Association) in 1863 aimed mainly at obtaining universal direct suffrage.]

The German State on a National and Socialist Foundation

In spite of their small number in relation to their host peoples they have been able to bring all important posts of public life into the hands of their Jewish racial comrades or of Germans closely related to Jews. But nevertheless a removal of the Jews from the German national body is completely possible – so much more so in that the real vitally important productive activity in industry and agriculture, in the professions and administration, is almost entirely free of Jews.

A removal of the Jews from our national body would neither disturb the agricultural production – I have not yet seen any Jew behind the plough going round the furrow – nor would the factories have to come to a standstill through lack of workers – the workforce will indeed know that no Jew hoists coal in hard work or stands at the forge – our work places of the smith and metalworker, carpenter and cobbler, would not be orphaned – the houses would not in any way have to remain as ruins after the expulsion of the Jews, the statistics do not mention anything of Jewish masons and carpenters, roofers or glazers. But even not in trade and commerce would a stagnation appear if the Jews were no longer there. In the field of the transport system, the state has already up to now taken care of personal and goods traffic in an exemplary way and, anyway, who has seen Jews as railway conductors or locomotive drivers – or as tram conductors, or as waggoners or transport workers?

But even in the field of the typical predisposition of the Jew to trade and finance, the military administrative posts before the war have shown that they were able to conduct a careful storage and provision service, in trade itself hundreds of thousands of commercial clerks and German businessmen are active who understand the real aspects and necessities of trade, and in the state bank and the postal bank we possess institutions that could form the basis of a healthy national economy freed of the Jewish robber economy.

If we have seen in this rather brief survey that the Jews represent in no way an irreplaceable function in our state and national life, that they, on the other hand, misuse their supremacy in the most ruthless way to the harm of their host peoples, then as an obvious and logical consequence is produced the demand for the expulsion of the Jews from our nation. Only one who pledges himself to the German national community can be a state citizen.

From this review of the racial question naturally and necessarily follow also the other consequences of the prohibition of the immigration of eastern Jews. It is a complete lack of understanding of the Jewish question if one believes that it is sufficient to repel the eastern Jews through a prohibition of immigration. It is absolutely necessary to simultaneously place the Jews hostile to our people settled amongst us under an aliens act. The eastern Jews are of course the great reservoir from which the Jews constantly replenish themselves. The great danger that this immigration includes in itself has been revealed with all clarity through the experiences of the last years. In a few years these eastern Jews have been able through all possible business tricks and flourishes to come into possession of enormous wealth. Our courtrooms are full of frauds exercised by such foreign elements. The state does not have the least interest in the immigration of such people who in no way make themselves useful productively.

This position of the National Socialist state to the eastern Jews does not exclude that even the members of other nations who are parasites on the national body can be expelled.

The discussion of these questions leads us now to the third section of the state policy of National Socialism: to the citizenship right.

The Citizenship Right

The citizenship right must be acquired. In this principle National Socialism differs considerably from the right valid at present according to which every adult German above 20 years, of male and female sex, can exercise state citizenship rights. Likewise today, according to the Weimar constitution, this possibility is open to the members of the Jewish race. Similarly this state membership can be acquired by any foreigner with the fulfilment of a few superficial formalities.

The Weimar constitution does not in general understand the concept of state citizen but speaks in Art.110 of membership in a state, and in Art.109 of equal rights before the law for all state members of male and female sex. The vagueness of this concept naturally excludes the demand of moral and racial preconditions for the acquisition of the citizenship right. In contrast to this, Art.113 of the Reich constitution takes the foreign-speaking "sections of the nation" (!) under its special protection; they "may not be disadvantaged in their free traditional development, especially in the use of their mother-tongue in education, as well as in the internal administration and administration of justice".

The German State on a National and Socialist Foundation

If one compares with this most comprehensive consideration of foreign nationals the practice of our Law for the Protection of the Republic against one's own national comrades, the obligation to deliver the so-called war-criminals to the enemy, with the certainty guaranteed in Art.112 that "no German of a foreign government may be delivered to persecution or punishment", and, if once compares precisely this last-mentioned article with the infamous judgements of the French against Krupp[61] and his directors, perhaps a reference to the fact that the author of this constitution was the Jew Preuss[62] suffices to set a definite light on all these events.

Not "the more fortunate future of the Poles", as Betthmann-Hollweg[63] said in one of his unfortunate parliamentary speeches, and not also the betterment of the Jews in Romania (according to Kühlmann)[64] can be the leading idea of a German state but only the welfare of the German people. This guiding theme is expressed in the national and economic programme of the NSDAP (The Programme, p.35) under No.7: "The rights and interests of the German precede those of the members of foreign nations" and under No.6: "One who is not a German can only live as a guest in Germany and stands under the aliens act".

According to this the state citizenship right must be acquired. It can also be lost through unworthiness. It is a right from which the Jews are fundamentally excluded, from which also members of other nations can be excluded.

The internal condition for the applicant for German state citizenship is the pledge to the German culture and community. One who

---

61 [Gustav Krupp von Bohlen und Halbach (1870-1950) ran the Friedrich Krupp AG from 1909 to 1941. In collaboration with the Reichswehr under Hans von Seeckt (1866-1936), Krupp undertook the secret rearmament of Germany in violation of the Treaty of Versailles. In 1923, when the French and Belgians occupied the Ruhr region, they also fined Krupp for holding a large public funeral for the thirteen workers of the Krupp factory in Essen shot dead by the French during the occupation.]

62 [Hugo Preuß (1860-1925) was the German-Jewish Minister of the Interior of the Weimar Republic and was instrumental in the formulation of the Weimar Constitution of 1919.]

63 [Theodor von Betthmann-Hollweg (1856-1921) served as German Chancellor from 1909 to 1917. During the war, Betthman-Hollweg seemed to be favouring more moderate policies than those advocated by the military leaders.]

64 [Richard von Kühlmann (1873-1948) served as Germany's Secretary of State for Foreign Affairs from August 1917 to July 1918. In May 1918 he negotiated the Peace of Bucharest with Romania.]

III. The State

does not pledge himself to the German nation in this way, one who declares himself to be an enemy of the German state, one who feels more closely bound to members of other nations than with his people, cannot receive any German state citizenship rights, for he indeed does not wish to have anything to do with the German community.

It seems to be indeed a madness when people who declare quite publicly that they know no fatherland called Germany, as Crispien[65] and others did, still wish to advise on the fate of this country, when they claim as representatives of the people, as delegates to still enjoy special privileges and when they still enjoy the protection of especially strict laws (the protection of the republic) in case they are promoted from this parliament to government positions.

The National Socialist German state will demand precisely from such men the hardest reckoning and the members of the revolutionary governments and parliaments will retrospectively have to take responsibility for their actions or omissions. The laws that are to be developed on the responsibility of all persons who stand in public life will therefore have to be endowed with retrospective powers.

Here it is not, as in the case of the mistake of the German revolution, a matter of the battle for wages of the hungry "proletarians" against the sated and insatiable capitalists, thus not about the misleading of the healthy and correct feelings of the working people through the idea of class-struggle, but here it is a matter of the moral demand that the irresponsibility of the present beneficiaries of the present parliamentary and government system must come to an end, and that those who have enriched themselves in an immoderate way on the need of the people or those who have abetted the machinations of other circles will be brought to the deserved punishment.

The slogan: "The little rogues are hanged, the big ones are allowed to go free" should not be proved right. The National Socialist state will, on the contrary, in the case of the determination of the punishment, take into consideration the fact of the small rogues' being seduced as a very mitigating one and, on the other hand, bring the big criminals against the German people to justice with the total strictness of the law.

---

65 [Arthur Crispien (1875-1946) was elected as Social Democratic member of parliament in 1920 and became co-chairman of the Sozialdemokratische Partei (SPD) in 1922.]

The German State on a National and Socialist Foundation

The purgative work of this state court cannot now in any way stop with those who first came to power with the revolution. It will also have to target those under the Imperial government who, through their negligence, made this German downfall possible. The chief responsible – Bethmann-Hollweg – has indeed been taken from his earthly judges, the same is true of the next most guilty – Erzberger,[66] who, as the father of the wretched parliamentary revolution of July 1917, raised once again the sinking will-to-win of the enemies. Even Eisner[67] and Rathenau have been removed from the scene of their nation-destroying activity, to be sure in an illegal way but according to the iron laws of history. But many of those still live who, through the organisation of the munitions strike in January 1918, thrust a dagger into the back of the fighting army, and those still live who through speech and writing broke the will to win, those still live who preached 'peace without winners and losers', those still live and accept it as right who misused the distress of the people in war and revolution for their own immoderate enrichment.

Certainly such a national political demand will spread fear and horror, and tens of thousands will fear for their lives because they are not of pure heart. But for National Socialism with this demand for social justice stands and falls the question of destiny for the German people, whether the German people can find its way to a noble nation, or whether it will eke out a miserable life in degradation and corruption as a fellaheen nation. For the National Socialist movement its raison-d'être is also decided by this question.

The state citizenship right is accordingly not a thing that will be placed in the cradle of everybody born in Germany; much rather, this state citizenship right includes in itself also the highest moral obligations towards the state and nation. The observance of this responsibility to

---

66 [Matthias Erzberger (1875-1921) was a member of the Deutsche Zentrumspartei (Catholic Centre Party) who was considered Betthman-Hollweg's right-hand man. During the war, in mid-1917, he urged a negotiated end to the war and undermined confidence in the German military. Erzberger signed the armistice ending the first World War and, as Finance Minister in the Weimar Republic, he endorsed the Treaty of Versailles. He was assassinated in 1921 by ultra-national members of the 'Organisation Consul' founded by the Freikorps commander, Hermann Ehrhardt (1881-1971).]

67 [Kurt Eisner (1867-1919) was a German Jewish socialist who organised the revolution that overthrew the Wittelsbach dynasty of Bavaria in November 1918. He became the republican prime minister of Bavaria and at the Berne Conference of Socialists he attacked the moderate socialists for not acknowledging Germany's guilt in bringing about the first World War. He was assassinated by the nationalist Count Arco von Valley in February 1919.]

the state and nation must however also be protected by the possibility that this right may again be lost in case of unworthiness.

On the other hand, the acquisition of the state citizenship right will not be an act of mercy but a claim that every industrious German can raise who proves himself worthy of the German community and who pledges himself to the German racial and historical community. One who has fulfilled his army and work obligation, one who is active as an honourable worker in his profession, has a claim to the acquisition of the state citizenship right.

But with this state citizenship right is also bound the obligation not to forget in all one's work the view of the larger whole and also to be always conscious in one's economic activity of the fact that one must fit one's work into the whole, that is, even with full freedom in particular areas, the activity of the German state citizen should not be directed against the welfare of the whole.

National Economy

The task of the national economy is the fulfilment of demand and not the attainment of as high an interest-yield for loan capital as possible.

One would think that this principle is taken for granted for every economy, and yet the National Socialist economy is different from the current interest capitalistic economy precisely in this guiding principle. It is not so easy for the guileless sense of the productive man to imagine a national economy that does not serve the fulfilment of demand; and yet it must be made clear now that for the current masters of the economy – the bank- and stock-exchange capital – the fulfilment of demand is basically of very little importance. International capital has an interest in it only insofar as this fulfilment of demand can be exploited in a usurious capitalistic way.

We have in fact to do here with two fundamentally different attitudes to the economy. The only urgent demand on the entire economy from the side of the entire population is, naturally, the satisfaction of the need for food, then the fulfilment of the demand for housing and clothing, and only then are ranged in an assortment all the other daily requisites up to the higher arts and cultural pleasures. In between come the support services, the entire transport system and whatever is connected with it, trade and the financial system. The production of goods for its part has in a healthy economy the worthiest goal of

The German State on a National and Socialist Foundation

covering the need in the best possible way through a payment which covers the production costs and includes a corresponding work-income for the entrepreneur and a suitable profit-share from which both unavoidable losses and improvements and renovations in the enterprise can be defrayed.

The attention of the just entrepreneur is not directed to the attainment of immoderate profit in individual cases, even when fortunate accidents might make this possible. The just entrepreneur is completely conscious of his national economic tasks, to establish production in such a way that the need can be covered with the least costs for the user, that at the same time the enterprise grows and flourishes, that the production costs become ever smaller without the wages being reduced.

Perhaps the most illuminating example of such a true way of entrepreneurial thought is Ernst Abbé,[68] the co-founder and director of the Zeiss works in Jena. This man has understood to a high degree of perfection this national economic task of the entrepreneur and sought to realise this to the best of his ability.

But in this respect we have also, in general no reason to make special complaints about our entrepreneurs before the war. Men like Alfred Krupp,[69] Mannesmann,[70] Werner Siemens,[71] Thyssen,[72] Borsig,[73] Krauss, Maffei,[74] etc. have secured for themselves even socially a place

---

68 [Ernst Abbé (1840-1905) was a physicist and entrepreneur who was hired by Carl Zeiss, the founder of the Jena company, Carl Zeiss AG that produced optical instruments and systems. Abbé became a co-owner of the firm.]

69 [Alfred Krupp (1812-1887) was the son of Friedrich Krupp (1787-1826), who had founded the Krupp Cast Steel Company in 1811. During Alfred Krupp's directorship, the company became the leading weapons manufacturing company of the age]

70 [Mannesmann was founded in 1890 and originally produced seamless steel tubes.]

71 [Werner Siemens (1816-1892) was an inventor and founder of the Telegraphen-Bauanstalt company in 1847. Today Siemens AG is one of the largest electro-technological companies in the world.]

72 [August Thyssen (1842-1926) founded the Thyssen-Foussol iron works in 1867 and acquired other heavy industrial companies which were amalgamated in 1926 into the Vereinigte Stahlwerke, the biggest mining and steel cartel in the world before the second World War.]

73 [Borsig was a locomotive company founded by August Borsig (1804-1854) in 1837.]

74 [Krauss-Maffei is a machine-producing company that was founded in 1838.]

III. The State

of honour in the history of German industry. They were all not ruled by one-sided pursuit of profit, they all remained simple and modest for themselves, only the prosperity of their works was their lodestar.

Indeed, the tireless productive and inventive power of the German industry has resulted in the fact that not only the gigantic increase in population found work and bread but that, in spite of rising wages, in spite of a comprehensives improvement of the standard of living of all sections of the population, the most important products could be made cheaper thanks to ever new improvements and inventions. The German manual worker should never forget that he owes this to the brain-workers.

And another thing must be stressed here again with all emphasis: that the foundation and precondition for this high blossoming of the German economy was the powerfully led Bismarck Reich. These two factors, the united and therefore powerful political situation of the German Reich and the unprecedented industriousness of the German entrepreneurs and workers made it possible that a comprehensive raising of the standard of living of the entire population was registered, that the gigantic increase in population of Germany could be fed, clothed and housed and that the emigration from Germany sank to insignificant numbers.

The numbers of the German migration in the decades after 1870 included only the healthy surplus of the German entrepreneurial and merchant spirit that streamed out into the world as the pioneers of German industriousness and German performance.

For the most part the entire national economy of the German Reich did justice to the fundamental demands that we too place on a healthy national economy.

The demand was amply covered. Nevertheless there appeared even at that time deep damages in our economy which were expressed in diverse ways.

1. Our state finances fell into ever greater debts at the same time in which the German people became ever richer and more powerful, in which the products of German industrial and trade efficiency conquered the sales markets of the world, at a time in which our internal economy strode from success to success and the medical and living conditions became better from year to year.

The German State on a National and Socialist Foundation

Now, it is naturally not a good sign if the debts become increasingly bigger. Such a phenomenon always points to the fact that something is not in order. For it must indeed be considered as fully absurd and nonsensical if a state whose citizens enjoy increasing wealth does not at the same time find itself in a condition of healthy and flourishing state finances. This must be so much more surprising when to the German Reich and the federal states extraordinarily large revenues flowed from their railways, post and mining works, as well as from the state forests, etc., quite apart from the fact that the Reich and the federal states could, by virtue of their financial sovereignty, claim the considerable tax capacity of their citizens.

2. A further deep-seated economic damage was the progressive debt of our agricultural and urban real estate. The movement of land reform that was applied against that correctly recognised a very important part of the entire problem without unfortunately achieving complete efficacy.

3. The fact of the inflation of our industry through credit of all sorts should also have filled sharp-sighted observers with anxiety. Certainly, in times of increasing prosperity the commercial and industrial enterprises take the acceptance of foreign monies and the interest obligation bound with that lightly, because indeed the strongly increased work and income possibility permits the bearing of these burdens. But woe if economic crises set in! Then the use of interest-bound credit shows itself in its entire economic banefulness.

The form of stock company that emerged in these years with the actual detachment of capital from work bound to it, that is, the separation of pure capitalistic interests in the profitability of money, on the part of the creditors, from the healthy cooperation of the individual entrepreneur and from the entire identification of his existence with his enterprise similarly sowed the seed of profound economic damages.

4. The growing position of power of the money-brokering institutes, the banks, should have filled the honourable friend of the nation with anxiety. From servants of the economy the banks became the unrestricted masters of the entire national economy. In a noteworthy and significant way this growing position of power of the banks was in no way accompanied by a concurrent prosperity of our national economy, but, on the contrary, the more lamentable our economy became the more the banks aggrandised themselves.

III. The State

We do not wish here to go further into this development, there will be much to say on it in the discussion of the purely financial- and monetary-economy. The mention of the fourfold root of the great national economic damage through the financial and credit system was of great importance because precisely this aspect of the entire economy has become the opposite of a true national economy, namely a one-sided robber economy of the financial powers.

One on whom the image of a body stricken with parasites does not spontaneously impose itself must be very interested in the retention of the present situation or dependent on the beneficiaries of this exploitative economy. Unfortunately, the last is the case among a very great number of men. That is why the internal resistance to this modern economic robber baron system does not emerge in a corresponding manner.

It is especially bad that even the science, and indeed especially the science, that has to deal with these things dutifully is still, with a few exceptions (Othmar Spann),[75] within the spell of the current interest capitalistic economy and finds itself in dependence on it. The present-day national economy is not a leader towards the truth and to right knowledge but has become the spokesman of national economic criminality.

All great truths and wisdom can be understood and contemplated in their essential aspects by every simple man. Not to be confused with this is the fact that it is naturally not so simple to arrive at such fundamental knowledge. To be sure, the knowledge itself, the intuition, is like a bright light that shines in the soul eternally thirsting for knowledge. Difficult however is the subsequent work of the understanding which must strenuously pile up brick upon brick in order to build up, with the most careful selection of materials, the entire thought-structure so that the finished work appears to everybody as self-evident.

In such cases there is then no finer praise than when one occasionally comes to such thoughts by oneself. Thus did I receive, while I was

---

75 [Othmar Spann (1878-1950) was an Austrian anti-Socialist economist and sociologist influenced by the economic theories of Adam Müller (1779-1829) - who had opposed Adam Smith's materialistic liberal economics. He was professor at the University of Vienna from 1919 until 1938, when he was barred from his professorship by the National Socialists after the Anschluss (annexation) of Austria. Although Spann sympathised with the nationalist orientation of the NSDAP, his views of a corporatist state were not entirely supported by the National Socialists.]

The German State on a National and Socialist Foundation

working on this work (Summer 1923), an excellent work of a now old man, the Austrian engineer W. Schober,[76] in which the entire disastrous development of the Austrian financial and credit situation was predicted with unprecedented clarity already 30 years ago.

Schober pointed to the fact that only a complete departure from the fundamentally false national economic doctrines could stop the disastrous development of the national economy – unfortunately without the least success.

The chief reason lay at that time in the fact that Schober's friends, of the Christian-Socialist Party, after an initial enthusiastic agreement, turned away from him with lazy excuses: "The time is not yet ripe", but in reality because it did not suit the Christian high finance.

The bank stopped a long time ago being the trusted intermediary between savings capital and the claims of the economy and the working capital. Today, the big banks have their directors and delegates sitting in all stock companies. Nothing can take place without the bank's knowing of it. And what interest does the bank now have in the economy? It has a sole interest in the capital yielding as high a profit as possible; in what way is quite indifferent to it. It does not see its task in the fertilisation of the economy through the loan of money at the cheapest rates precisely when the national economy is threatened by crises of the worst sort – this however would be its highest task –; the big banks much rather tend to come forth precisely at that time with credit packages and credit notices when the manufacturing industry most urgently needs an anticipatory credit for its work.

One may further consider the following: What need do the banks cover? - One will say: the need for money. Of course. But how and under what conditions? The baker, the shoemaker, the factory owner, the businessman, indeed cover the real need of food, clothing, etc., and they receive for that the equivalent value, the price, in money or through a transfer of money. Therewith the need is covered, and the factory owner, etc. has again working capital for purchases, payment of wages, and further manufacture. Here we see an economic circle

---

76 [Wenzel Schober (1846-1928) was an Austrian railway engineer who - like the Viennese professor Josef Schlesinger (1830-1901) - identified in his economic writings the dependence on Jewish international finance as the chief cause of the economic problems of Austria. His major works included *Die Noth und ihre Ursachen*, 3 vols., Vienna, 1880-82, and *Die Valuta-Regulierung in Österreich*, 1892.]

III. The State

completed. The producer covers the need of the user, the money fulfils its proper task as the intermediary of an exchange business and fertilises anew the economy in the hands of the producer.

It is quite different in the case of the money-lending business. First, there does not exist for any bank any obligation to give away its ware – money - the way such an obligation exists, for example, for every trader. It can therefore ensure that it gives money to only those who are favourable to it. Further, the bank demands, in the largest number of cases, securities that far exceed the value of the loan, it demands further a debt certificate according to which the debtor must pledge himself to the repayment of the debt with everything that he has and will earn. In other words, against the dispensing of money the bank draws into its power-domain assets that are far greater than the loaned sum; it also lets a debt certificate be handed out which exposes the work incomes of the debtor to its grasp. But that is not enough: for this doubly, and many times, secured loan of money, the bank lets itself be paid still more in the form of interests that become enormous over time. We thus have to do here with a procedure which, considered economically, is not a productive performance at all, the return payment – pledge, debt certificate – is given immediately, and, besides that, the debtor must agree to another continuing payment which in a few years exceeds the value of the received money, without the pledger becoming free or the debt being resolved. Such a financial business is naturally national economically an absurdity, it is unadulterated usury.

The true sense of credit, of the belief in the greater economic efficacy of another, is indeed that the owner of saved money does not see that he is in a position to use his money himself in a profitable way, he therefore turns to someone whom he can trust that he can entrust this money to and who offers him the guarantee that he will again return his savings to him at request fully and undiminished. If the loan strengthens the debtor in his economic work capacity that he could make considerably greater profits one can consider this as an act of fairness or gratitude if the debtor gives the creditor, apart from the return of the money, also a certain share of his profits. This conception of private monetary- and credit economy rules the entire Middle Ages, it formed the core of the Church's doctrine of interest. The demand of interest was considered as usury. Today, the interest that was judged to be usury by the Church has become indeed axiomatic of our entire economy – the national economic sense of credit has become a national economic nonsense. To be sure, for the moneyed man such a doctrine is the source of lasting effortless enrichment. Not really because gold is – as it would like to appear – really a power that produces money from itself, a superhuman phenomenon that, freed from the earthly laws of perishability, forces everything under its spell imperishably and forever, but because it is felt in modern financial and international economics simply as a law that every sort of financial possession bears in itself a claim to interest, to a certain degree innate in money, is this most monstrous reversal of the relation between work and money accepted as a law, as something that cannot be touched, as something for which the science dealing with it has to produce a great number of justifying reasons.

Only in this way was it possible to divert the entire national economy from its sole and natural task of covering the need and therewith creating work and food for everybody and to misuse it primarily as an instrument for the personal enrichment of the owners of bank- and stock-exchange capital.

It is now a favourite trick of the political battle against our movement that this opposition of ours against the high capitalistic exploitation of our national economy and our battle for a national economy satisfying the demands of social justice is portrayed as an opposition between property and other forms of possession, that our demand "Public interest before self-interest" is decried as Communistic. Against this, we should constantly point to Art.8 of the national and economic programme (The Programme, p.35):

> "National Socialism fundamentally recognises private property and places it under government protection".

It will however be the task of the legislation to draw the limits with regard to the hoarding of immoderate wealth in the hands of individuals at the expense of the whole.

Positively and for the economy itself there arises, as a demand for the entire economy and its tasks in the spirit of National Socialism, demand No.10 of the "National and Economic Programme": All Germans form a work community for the promotion of the common welfare and culture of the German people.

From here is derived in turn the moral demand that every German must work intellectually and physically according to his strength, but that this work of his must be incorporated into the whole.

III. The State

I stress that this is a moral demand. It is a matter therefore not of the establishment of a compulsion to work as has been introduced in Soviet Russia. Something quite different is the introduction demanded by us of a year of compulsory work for every German before the acquisition of full state citizenship rights.

It is again quite different that our main goal aims precisely at securing a worry-free old age for all national comrades who have worked industriously in their youthful and adult years. Precisely in the case of a national economy which does not stand continuously under the blood-letting of an interest- and toll obligation to loan capital it will, and must and can, be easily achieved that it gives away large surpluses in such a way that to all national comrades a suitable and adequate old age pension – similar to the retirement pay of officials – is ensured on reaching a certain age or in the case of a work disability that has occurred prematurely.

I bring in this social political demand here because the fulfilment of this task belongs to the performances of the entire national economy, because it is the point that is not only able to say constantly to the worker in the widest sense of the word: You must work!, but because, behind the work compulsion, it establishes something comforting and reconciling – the prospect of a secured old age for everybody who has done his duty all his life long.

Within the scope of the fundamental recognition of private property as the foundation of our economy belongs naturally also the fact that every German is protected in his free possibility of earning a living and in the free disposal of his work-income and his acquired wealth (No.11 of the "National and Economic Programme"). Limiting this basic right is only permissible through the law, whereby the guideline should be followed that only such work is considered as work that is not directed against the interests of the community. Chain-trade and profiteering also doubtlessly cause much work; similarly, a burglar will often shed more drops of sweat in his "work" than the mason in the building of a house, but such "work" is directed indeed only to one-sided personal enrichment at the cost and harm of others. Such "work" is therefore generally harmful and must therefore be punished with all severity.

Such an express determination is in no way superfluous for, from the practice of the law is apparent all too often, and to a frightful extent, how many things are designated there as honest work. There is also an

The German State on a National and Socialist Foundation

entire series of activities which are very close to the border-line, where it is difficult to say that this work still harmonises "with the whole".

In any case, legal tools must be created so that all these activities or enterprises that are directed against the national health in a physical or intellectual way may be suppressed. The same is true of the exploitation of the distress of the population through profiteering and usury.

For such vermin that are hostile to the nation we demand the death penalty. Financial penalty or even imprisonment is ineffective against such unscrupulous people.

In short therefore the economic policy of National Socialism will work towards removing a basically false concentration of economics on profitability and for that reason to restore to honour the only right and reasonable task of national economics: the fulfilment of demand.

This does not in any way exclude income and profit for the trader, factory owner and the honest businessmen; on the contrary, in no way should difficulties be created for the justified striving for earnings so long as this striving is contained within the scope of the public interests.

It is a matter therefore of a purgative action, and then of the maintenance of the German economy which is unobjectionable both in relation to its forms and with respect to its performances. By this is to be understood what No.12 of the "National and Economic Programme" demands: The healthy combination of big-, medium- and small businesses in all fields of the economic life, thus also in agriculture, remains upheld.

Therewith is also given the fundamental position of National Socialism to the different social orders.

National Socialism will support and promote agriculturists through all means as the foundation of a powerful nation and of the nourishment of the population.

If point 17 of the Programme contains a clause which envisages a free dispossession in special circumstances, by this was only meant, as Adolf Hitler proclaimed on April 13, 1928, the "creation of legal possibilities of confiscating if necessary land that was acquired in

III. The State

an illegal way or not administered according to the viewpoint of the welfare of the people. This is directed thus mainly against the Jewish land speculation companies". This clause was therefore designed only for the protection of the native population.

Especially dear to National Socialism lies also the prosperity and the independence of a healthy commercial and mercantile middle class.

And even in the forms of production of the so-called heavy industry there is, from the point of view of National Socialism, nothing essential to be objected to. Precisely this large industry has rationalised everything in an exemplary way, that is, it has avoided no costs to bring about better and simpler production methods. The present overburdening of enterprises - aiming at communisation - with an excessive number of people who are really dispensable (we are thinking here mainly of the necessity of maintaining one's own tax- and insurance officers, etc.) naturally works directly against the nationalisation effort of industry.

At the conclusion of these economic political tasks of National Socialism stands another enormous organisational performance: "The introduction of a year of work-service for every German".

Even here it is a deeply moral principle that compels this demand – duty.

One who wishes to exercise state-citizenship rights must have also served the state, he must also have proved himself duty-conscious and loyal to his state through deed and indeed without remuneration, that is, possibility of enrichment, exactly as the soldier serves his fatherland.

We glimpse in the idea of the compulsory work service a fully supplementary idea to the idea of universal military service.

As much as we would like to consider it possible to substantially reduce the training to become efficient soldiers compared to the earlier two- and three-year long service period, so much do we consider it necessary and advisable that every young German be acquainted with one or more commercial activities in which he can serve the state.

The duty-consciousness with regard to the quality of work has suffered so much under the rule of the machine and under the still more

The German State on a National and Socialist Foundation

devastating doctrine of the class hostility of the workers against the entrepreneurs that a tutoring in this field under tight state direction according to uniform principles seems completely indispensable. Precisely the entrepreneurs, in the good sense, will welcome such an institution and not consider it in any way as a competition. Such a work-army cannot be a competition already because, according to experience, every productive economic activity of the state must be excessively burdened with its official apparatus, because the employment and training of a young inexperienced workforce consumes too much of its efficiency.

On the other hand, it will be the task of this year of work-service to better acquaint the young people in model state enterprises with all the progresses of technology. They should, if possible, cover the actual needs of the workforce and of the national comrades serving militarily.

Thus a state competition with the rest of the national economy does not come into question, it could at most operate in certain fields as a price regulator with market prices that still leave to the free tradesmen and the free entrepreneurs a wide scope for a reasonable profit.

It cannot be the task of this manifesto to go further into details. Nevertheless they must be sketched and illuminated briefly, for we know that a correct solution of this question will be of enormous advantage for the recovery of our economic morale, quite apart from the benefit that the entire economy will derive from the fact that the idea of duty with regard to work will be awakened as a moral duty with regard to the nation.

With respect to the position of the state-citizen with regard to the national economy Bismarck once declared:

"We do not live to be happy but to do our duty."

This moral principle lies also at the basis of our position with regard to the state and the economy.

III. The State

National Financial Reform
Money And Credit In The National Socialist State

The Rule Of Interest

The demand for the breaking of the interest-slavery is groundbreakingly new in a political programme. This fact alone would be enough for the widest circles to bring forward a most vehement opposition to National Socialism.

By far the largest part of the opponents is constituted of those who have indeed lost everything through the present interest capitalistic economy and who, brought up in these ideas, still fear the loss of already lost privileges. This opposition indeed possesses no impetus, for precisely the lack of any internal impetus is characteristic of the circle trapped in the capital pension ideal.

A further group is those who are dependent on loans or at least believe that they are. This group naturally fears not really the abolition of the obligation to pay interest but it fears that it would not receive any more working capital unless everything remains as before.

Another group is the wonderful national economists for whom opposition to the problem of the liberation from interest is the alpha and omega of their national economic wisdom.

A further group is the malicious who are indeed not of a better viewpoint but who, for personal or party tactical reasons, combat this basic demand of National Socialism with false assertions and misrepresentations.

That the circles of international finance exercising the rule of interest are, precisely on account of this demand, our most irreconcilable and bitter enemies is self-evident.

With the exception of the malicious and the professionally interested opposition the chief reasons for a hostile and mistrustful attitude are – ignorance and intellectual laziness, stupidity.

We have to do here with quite powerful opponents, with opponents among whom any system that one may try to enforce fails, who draw back like jelly-fish from the pressure of convincing explanations but immediately after the relaxation of the pressure flow back once again into the old ways of thought.

So what is understood by "interest slavery"? By interest slavery is to be understood the interest-bound debt of the state and people to the supranational financial powers. Here therefore it is a matter of a new form of slavery, of the slavery to the rule of finance. This slavery is more frightful and cruel than any form of rule ever was under the rule of absolute princes, because it is exercised in an impersonal way, without any human feeling, obsessed only with an insatiable instinct to expand and enlarge, with a greed for power without comparison.

The customary expression for the existence of this rule is: "Money moves the world". But here money is only used as a symbol of mastery for financial power. Money itself, the metal and paper currencies, are in themselves naturally neither good nor bad, and exercise no sort of rule. Money as a currency is indispensable for the exchange of goods and services. That is why all attempts to deal with the rule of the financial powers from the side of money alone are from the start erroneous and doomed to ineffectiveness, because in the case of this rule we are not indeed dealing with a question of the narrow monetary system but with questions of power. Money as an instrument of power is in itself, as mentioned, neither good nor bad, it depends only on its use. The fact that it can be also be used murderously, that is, misused does not in any way neutralise its endlessly various and indispensable useful usage possibilities. Even money, applied in a useful way, has a beneficial effect on the national economy. Money has not wrongly been called the blood in the national economic body. So long as money remains true to its task as a means of exchange, so long as money received or earned is again directed back to the economy, it cannot exercise any harmful influence on the national economy.

Now there comes in a factor: that is the desire to use money as a savings method. This desire is itself completely justified, on the contrary, it is only to be fully wished that the savings sense may be restored to honour again if - yes, if - savings were indeed possible at all in the present-day circumstances. The lasting, threatening devaluation of our German money through an irresponsible State financial policy indeed makes saving a stupidity, for, after a few weeks or days, the value of the money can have sunk to a fraction of its earlier value. Therefore if money should fulfil its task as savings money, it must be of stable value.

III. The State

Since the German money, for reasons that we shall still have to investigate, is not of stable value at the moment and also cannot be of stable value, the German saver looks around in every unstable period for such money of stable value. Such a money of stable value is the so-called noble currencies, the dollars, the Swiss francs and Dutch gulden, the monies of the Scandinavian peoples, etc., as well as the metallic money from precious metals.

But now the national economic task of money as the working capital of the economy stands opposed to this desire for accumulation of stable money. To understand this question in its entire depth we must adhere to the fact that money according to its essence is and should be nothing but a "token of performed work". The customary explanation: 'Money is a means of exchange' is in no way false, but it does not exhaust the question. It is a task of money, and indeed its most important one, to mediate the exchange of goods. But this task is fulfilled also by other things like the tea-packets of the Chinese, the cowry shells of the negroes, etc. The innermost essence of the money dispensed by the state today, as well as of the money surrogates, is that they are tokens – one could also say vouchers – of some work performed by other persons. By "performed work" we must understand quite comprehensively every economic product, thus also raw materials, for even these have commercial or sales value only if they are quarried and if they are brought to the market. In order to facilitate this exchange of goods among themselves, indeed in order to make this possible at all in a complicated economy, a means of exchange had to be invented which would directly make it possible that the producer of only one ware would be able to satisfy his own manifold needs through this means of exchange, which had a general validity. A cobbler makes shoes and boots year in, year out – but he needs his daily bread, meat, milk, eggs, he needs clothing and so on. The baker, from whom the cobbler buys his bread, may indeed need one or two pairs of boots in a year, but he cannot really be paid the whole year through for all the bread that everybody eats with only boots, he must indeed also pay his miller and firewood supplier for flour and fuel, but these can also not use any more boots because they themselves already get boots and shoes from another cobbler. But the baker cannot naturally pay the miller for his flour with his own products, the baker must bake bread for the community. In other words: a pure exchange economy is quite impossible in a developed national economy with an extensive division of labour. An exchange intermediary is therefore indispensable. In the most general form this exchange intermediary must be a generally recognised record, protected by the state, of the productions of the national economy; one must also be able to buy something with these records and everybody must be obliged to provide his commercial products for this exchange money.

It is, for example, also erroneous to say that money is a record of a performed work. Certainly, one accepts this money as a performed work, but not because an economic cycle is already completed therewith but because this money is indeed a record of every one of many performed work-activities – records with which everybody can satisfy his requirement for life-necessities and his other needs. Only when this need is covered and the money is fed back into the economy is the basic cycle of money completed. But if the money remains lying as hoarded or saved money in one hand, then only half an exchange, only half a cycle is executed. The money has not yet fulfilled its goal, on the contrary, it has been withdrawn from the goal for which it was invented and for which it exists. We must fundamentally declare that this interruption of the national economic task of money is, for national economic and national political reasons, impermissible. It obviously cannot be that every financial amount received must be immediately given out, that the financial market must be provided so abundantly with money that every private person can make his economic arrangements in such a way that he preserves for himself sums for the covering of his monthly requirements or the amounts for larger one-time yearly services, but it must be declared as completely inadmissible national economically that the currency dispensed by the state for the welfare of the community is withdrawn from the public circulation as hoarded money.

To the financial system therefore corresponds also the duty to spend, that is, the duty to bring acquired money back into circulation.

One may also specify here again quite sharply that savings is therewith in no way made impossible. Savings, understood rightly, is in no way the avaricious and miserly hoarding of money but – if one wishes to employ the favourite combination of the idea of savings with children's relief - , it is the creation and acquisition of goods, the purchase or building of a small house, the purchase of valuable objects, of collections, books, pictures, household goods, the expansion and improvement of the business establishment, the extension of the stocks, etc., and that is a far better "savings" than the hoarding of gold.

Precisely we Germans have had to undergo an education in world-view of the grandest style on this question. This correct "savings" just

III. The State

described has rewarded itself best, the false one focussed on money has been bitterly avenged.

This unerringly correct feeling of the people even for these matters has been reflected quite correctly in sagas and fairy-tales. The hoarded money is transformed into worthless clod or it disappears, or it brings endless misfortune. On the other hand, always and everywhere, the one who, out of his industriousness, has "achieved something" - and by that healthy reasoning always understands a blooming private economy, be it mercantile, commercial or industrial - has acquired respect and esteem. Such a development of wealth is unobjectionable, it is not directed against the spirit of money, it is, as a thriving member of the entire economy, social in the best sense.

After these brief but necessary, because essential, observations on the financial system let us return to the point of departure of our question: "What do we mean by interest-slavery.?"

If, through the withholding of money in the hands of people who are not conscious of the national economic task of money, or still more in the hands of those who wish to use the collected money as an instrument of power, a deadlock arises, the money that remains in circulation becomes scarcer, there appears a money squeeze. But those who possess money still do not, in a national economically healthy manner, put their money back into circulation because they for their part satisfied continuing needs and had houses built or purchased other commercial or industrial products. They therefore do not take away from the businessman or the factory owner, who definitely needs the working capital for the maintenance of his enterprise, his products but they give him the money withheld by them illegitimately, in a national economic sense, against a special toll – against interest. The national economic squeeze begins.

The relation of the production of goods – the producer – of the national economic worker to money is at one stroke turned upside down. The money that was, according to its essence and its invention, to serve the economy has suddenly emancipated itself and exercises a squeeze on the production of goods. The financial rule begins. Certainly the private economy is glad that it can maintain its enterprises at least in this way, for it feels itself bound to serve production national economically. The money hoarder derives from this feeling of national economic duty of the national economic worker a double benefit: first he has a debt certificate drawn up – thus a legal title – according to which the debtor with his entire wealth is liable for the undiminished repayment of the loaned sums, in most cases other definite objects of wealth are quite especially pledged, and secondly, the debtor must pledge himself further to a continuous extra payment which one calls interest.

The guaranteed credit is thus not given for reasons which would correspond to the literal sense of the word credit, that is, to the trust in the greater economic efficacy and performance capacity, but purely with the intention of exploiting the need of the economic entrepreneur to procure for oneself without any effort a part of his work-income. The credit is also not given to therewith promote production, but solely to make the possession of money "profitable". To what businesses the credit is used is basically a matter of complete indifference to the creditor; if he is interested in it, this happens only in order to assure himself that his money is safe and, above all, that it is also effectively interest-bearing.

Observed generally, the credit system that is mediated by the banks is today built up in such a way that generally the capitalist, the possessor of money and credit, is fully detached from work. He has no relationship at all of a personal nature to the different branches of production in which he "lets his money work", as the favourite misleading expression goes. What does the share-holder know of "Girmes", "Pöge", "Weser", "Riebeck Montan", "Otavi", "Salitrera", "Steaua Romana",[77] what does he know what is manufactured in these works? He does not have any interest in it, he has only the one-sided interest whether the shares rise or fall, and how high the dividends are that his capital yields. It is also a matter of complete indifference whether the stock companies or the other forms of capitalistic activity (joint-stock company, society with limited liability, union, etc.) serve production in general. The main thing, the only decisive thing is – the "profitability". A proof of the fact is the enormous popularity that the bank shares enjoy. The big banks, as well as every credit institution, perform in general no productive work in the sense of the production of goods. Here, in the big bank system, the idea of interest - that is, the possibility of transferring a gigantic share of the incomes of productive work

---

77 [Girmes is a textile company founded by Johannes Girmes (1854-1912); Weser was a ship-building company, Riebeck-Montan was a mining company, Otavi was a mining and railway company, Salitrera was a Chilean saltpetre company, Steaua Romana is a Romanian oil-refining company.]

III. The State

into the possession of the mere money-owner, and indeed, for the latter, completely effortlessly - celebrates real orgies. Today there is almost no more enterprise that is not dependent in some form on the bank, that is not run in a purely interest-capitalistic form. The entire national economic work is dependent on the bank- and stock-exchange capital and interest-bound to it.

The lords of the banks – the high finance – are therewith also the lords of production. It is dependent on them whether the work comes to a stop or whether the market is deluged with an enormous amount of rubbish. For the organised private sector the fulfilment of demand is totally an incidental matter.

In the case of this interest capitalistic economic form of the modern credit system we thus have to do with the most complete national economic immorality, with a total perversion of the meaning of the financial and credit system as of a servant of the economy into the position of absolute lord of the economy.

Creative and productive work has become the slave and the cunningly rapacious, eternally mobile Jewish spirit of usury rules the world. A piece of extortion only possible through the conjuring up of an artificial state of emergency through a national economically illegitimate withholding of money. And that is considered today as just, as a right nobody dares touch because it brings him into conflict with the world-ruling power of large loan capital.

The slavery to interest has been perfected!

It was perfected through the fact that the seductive arts of the mobile spirit succeeded in tying even the state, the given protector of the financial system, to the interest slavery so that it too, with bound hands, acknowledges international capital as its lord and has allowed itself to be diverted from its actual task as the protector of the national economy into the position of the bailiff, the interest-collector for large loan capital.

The National Financial Economy

It is now our special task to trace this development of the national financial economy.

The German State on a National and Socialist Foundation

Even here it will be the right way to start from a determination of the facts as they are found today.

The outstanding phenomenon in the national life of the nations of the western cultural circle is the enormous debt of all the states. Whether victor or vanquished, all bear gigantic debt burdens in their national economies affected severely by the war.

The most significant statistical work of the British Empire is The Statesman Yearbook; this official national yearbook gives for the individual states a precise overview of the condition of their public debts, etc.

According to it, the debt of England – that is, of the English working class – to international capital – on March 31, 1930, was 7,596,000,000 pounds sterling with a yearly interest payment of around 350 million pounds sterling. It is quite useful to convert this sum into German marks, since one sees best in this way that in this interest question it is a matter of an international question of the widest scope.

France owes to its internal and foreign interest creditors around 279 billion gold francs.

The United States of North America, the blessed land of the dollar, bears a public debt burden of around 16 billion dollars.

In Canada, Australia, India, Italy, Czechoslovakia, Poland, everywhere we find the same miserable picture of a hopeless debt of the states and, therewith, of the peoples to international capital. Everywhere the national life revolves around one question: How do we pay the interest for our loans, that is, for our debts to international finance, to the large loan capital?

The finance ministries in all states are relentlessly occupied in tapping new tax sources, the parliaments advise for months on the new tax bills, but all resistance is useless. Before the majesty of the international usurious capital and its chartered "legal" claims to the interest payments parliaments and governments collapse over and over again and oppress their peoples with unprecedented tax burdens, instead of their daring to put an end to this enormous international fraud with a flat 'No'.

III. The State

Injustice Became The Law, The Lord A Slave

How things stand in our poor fatherland we experience daily and hourly.

Violently and powerfully did the young German work-giant rise up after he had achieved a national unity through blood and iron. His tireless work, his creative spirit brought ever new inventions. The German entrepreneurial spirit and daring conquered the markets of the world. With amazed anxiety the French and English loan capital of the Rothschilds and the other bank magnates, as well as the trust capital of the American financial people, the Kahns, Loebs, Speyers, etc, saw itself threatened most seriously in its profitability. The value of the German mark, that is the quality and cheapness of German products, continued to rise, one could figure out when the mark would reach the value of the dollar until the English world trade would be surpassed by by Germany, one saw how all over the world the German transport installations, the German educational institutions, the German sanitational organisations, the German urban administrations, the German military methods were taken as a model, one saw how everywhere in the world German engineers as pioneers of German work capacity built railways, bridges and streets. But all this meant that the profitability of the capital loaned out all over the world by international finance was threatened. Then did international finance decide, with the help of international Freemasonry, to encircle Germany and, through the use of all the means of lies and slander, to represent Germany as the enemy of the world. - Edward VII was a only a piece pushed forward in this chess game. The nationalist passions were stoked against Germany, in England as well as in France. Indicating the political prehistory of the world war does not belong here, but it is in any case certain that Germany's side, in spite of its military strength, was lost, because there cannot in general be any talk of a political counter-game against the game of intrigue of the Entente powers (cf. Rosenberg, International Freemasonry).[78]

Even the only group that still had a foreign political instinct in

---

78 [Alfred Rosenberg published a work entitled *Das Verbrechen der Freimaurerei* (1921), as well as *Freimaurerische Weltpolitik* im Lichte der kritischen Forschung (1929) in the Nationalsozialistische Bibliothek series, vol.9.]

The German State on a National and Socialist Foundation

Germany, the All German,[79] did not have any idea that this powerful struggle between the armed nations was not about political success but was directed to the goal of the financial subjection of the German workers to the interest slavery of international capital. The militaristic overpowering of Germany was naturally France's special goal, the destruction of the German navy the special goal of England, but above both these imperialistic goals of France and England stood always the striving for world-rule of international capital.

While thus the nations tore one another apart in wild struggle and the blood of the best flowed in streams on the battlefields, Jewry of the entire world was in movement. For All-Judah the harvest time had come.

High finance financed the world war; in all the nations of the world the Jewish scribes sat in the editorial offices of the international press and lied to and instigated the nations to ever new efforts against one another. 26 states were in this way led into the war against the Central Powers. From the east there flowed in a stream of eastern Jews over the German lands; these thrust themselves forward, haggled and hogged and enriched themselves, took possession of the flats in the cities and acquired everything that they could get. In the military industrial companies this business of the plundering and misrule of the German workforce was taken care of by the members of the Jewish race, and the Jews forced themselves forward and up into all positions of the state and economy. The internal demoralisation was likewise consciously led by Jews, the Haases, Dittmanns, Cohns, Luxemburgs, Barths, then the Parvus-Helphands, Eisners, Leviens, Gradnauers[80]

---

79 [The Alldeutscher Verband was a German nationalist organisation founded in 1891. During the first World War, the association promoted German expansionist goals and, after the war, it supported general Erich Ludendorff (1865-1937) in his claim that Germany had been betrayed ("stabbed in the back") in the war by socialists and democrats.]

80 [Hugo Haase (1863-1919) was a Jewish socialist who became chairman of the Socialdemokratische Partei Deutschlands (SPD), along with the German August Bebel, in 1911. He professed to be a pacifist and organised a huge anti-war rally in July 1914.

Wilhelm Dittmann (1874-1954) was a prominent member of the SPD who was sentenced to imprisonment for his participation in the Berlin armament workers' strike in February 1918. During and after the November Revolution following the end of the first World War, Dittmann played an active parliamentary role as member of the Independent Social Democratic Party of Germany (USPD). In 1933, after Hitler's rise to power, Dittmann fled to Switzerland.]

Oskar Cohn (1869-1934) was a Jewish politician who worked with Karl

III. The State

agitated and incited, supported by ambitious people, fools and power-hungry criminals against the German people.

In this way did the German nation finally collapse from inside. Judah's star rose blood-red. The last nation that had firmly resisted the international finance and its witchcraft collapsed, it threw down its arms and bowed before the frightful yoke of the Versailles dictate. Bleeding from a thousand wounds, leaderless, not really on account of the expulsion of the princes, for precisely these had fully failed as real leaders, the German nation was led by its parliaments and parliamentary governments with the fateful sentence that can always be applied at such times, with the phrase, "To avoid worse", into the interest-slavery to loan capital.

Liebknecht, the founder of the Spartacist League, and was a staunch Zionist. He fled to Paris in 1933.

Rosa Luxemburg (1871-1919) was a Jewish Marxist who founded, along with Liebknecht, the Spartacist League which eventually became the Communist Party of Germany (KPD). Both Luxemburg and Liebknecht were assassinated by the Freikorps in 1919.

Emil Barth (1879-1941) joined the USPD in 1917 and one of the six members of the Council of deputies of the people (Rat der Volksbeauftragten) set up in November 1918 after the fall of the German monarchy (the other members being Friedrich Ebert, Philipp Scheidemann and Otto Landsberg of the SPD and Haase and Dittman of the USPD.]

Alexander Parvus (né Israel Helfand) (1867-1924) was a ghetto Jew from Belarus who was instrumental in effecting the Marxist strategy of a "permanent revolution" through his various international contacts with Rosa Luxemburg, Lenin, Trotsky and the Young Turks.

Max Levien (1885-1937) was a Russian Jewish Bolshevik who became a German citizen in 1913 and member of the KPD (Communist Party of Germany). In April 1919, Levien established the Bavarian Soviet Republic along with another Russian Jewish member of the KPD, Eugen Leviné (1883-1919). But this 'Soviet' experiment was put down by President Friedrich Ebert, who employed the Freikorps to maintain order in Munich. Leviné was arrested and executed by the Freikorps in May 1919, but Levien fled to Austria and the Soviet Union, where he too was executed in 1937 during Stalin's Great Purge.

Georg Gradnauer (1866-1946) was a Jewish member of the SPD who served as the first Minister-President of Saxony after the abolition of the Kingdom of Saxony. A moderate socialist, he attempted to quell the radicals in Leipzig with the help of the Freikorps, following the example of Ebert in Munich. This cost him electorally and he was forced to resign in 1920.]

The German State on a National and Socialist Foundation

The Versailles Dictate

The Dawes Pact and the Young Plan

The goal of the world war had been reached: Germany, the most industrious and efficient nation of the world removed as a competitor on the world market, militarily overpowered, made leaderless and seduced and poisoned by the false Marxist doctrines, morally dissipated and buried under a mountain of debts that it can never again remove from itself, but had to serve for ever as an interest slave to international capital.

According to the London payment plan, Germany has had to acknowledge an interest-bearing debt of 132 billion gold marks, and to this debt was added also the interests.

It would be ridiculous if it were not so frightfully serious and if the enemies did not take it so mercilessly precisely contrary to all the platitudes of the pacifists, "but it will not be so bad", and "reasonableness will triumph". No! It will not triumph! And the international finance will do everything to keep Germany continuously in this interest slavery. Only we can free ourselves.

It is the deep tragedy of the German nation that, as efficient as it in general is in its narrow work circle, it immediately becomes uncertain when it raises its glance beyond the limits of the daily work and stands before the great world occurrences. Here the conscientious and precise German loses all measure, he becomes a visionary and enthusiast. The "German professor", who performs outstanding things in his specialisation becomes, faced with the things of the world, an object of the comic papers, from the forgetting of his umbrella to the gushing prolixity of the ideologues; the German officer, trusting in the excellent efficiency of his troops, is inclined to underestimate the spiritual imponderables of a political nature and the power of ideas, and thereby to place the final success in doubt; the German official tends to think of himself as a boss of the population instead of as the servant of the whole.

So we see in great and small this disastrous trait in the German character: the Germans are specialists and dreamers. Individually more efficient and industrious in all special fields than any people, even completely capable of becoming enthusiastic about any great idea and with heroic bravery giving their life for an idea, but less skilled in

III. The State

seeing and hitting on the right solution within the intervening circle of international economic and political matters.

The reflection of such a fundamental character-trait in the German in the political field is his so oft lamented lack of national feeling and his political incompetence. The average German lacks to a certain degree the sense of large orderings; thus he also does not mostly understand that those debt figures are really his destiny, that those figures, that the acknowledgement of this debt and the willingness and the attempt to pay this debt in money and material goods is the basic reason for the entire desperate situation of the German nation. Much less does he see, however, that the beneficiaries of this German payment obligation are not really the other nations but solely – international finance.

To international finance, however, the repayment of the loan is in no way important, only the lasting obligation to interest. That and that alone is why international finance, which composed the Versailles dictate in its financial parts, set the basic sum so fantastically high from the start that a repayment can never be thought of but, even in an eventual reduction of the basic sum (in any case only with a simultaneous raising of the interest rate), Germany will permanently be held in interest-slavery.

The imposition of this interest rule over our poor industrious people was the final goal of the world war, it was the goal of high finance and this goal has been fully reached.

The relevant clauses of the Versailles dictate are so frightful, they show so clearly the entire seriousness and the destructive hardness of this interest rule which delivers everything that we have and that we work for to the grasp of international finance that I cite them in excerpts in the following:

Art.231. The Allied and associated governments declare, and Germany acknowledges (!), that Germany and its allies are, as the originators (!), responsible for all the losses and damages that the Allies and associated governments and their members have suffered as a result of the war forced upon them by the attack of Germany and its allies.

Although it is quite cynically acknowledged in Art.232 "that Germany's resources are not sufficient to ensure the complete restitution of all these losses and damages", the obligation is nevertheless demanded "that all these losses and damages be compensated".

Art.233 says: "The extent of the damages will be determined by the Reparations Commission.

Art.234 says: "The Reparations Commission will periodically test the payment capacity of Germany ... But it cannot waive any amount without the approval of the different governments represented in the Commission".

Art.234 determines: "Germany will pay before the determination of the final amount of the compensation claim ... 20 billion marks in gold (in gold, goods, ships, securities or in other ways)"

Germany will besides issue the bonds indicated in Art.12c of Annex II.

And now comes, prettily stowed away and near the end in this Annex II Art.12c in Section VIII of the so-called Versailles Peace Treaty, the financial political strangulation of Germany. This Art.12 says in its most important points as follows:

> The Commission has all powers and exercises all authority that are guaranteed to it in this treaty.
>
> The Commission has, in general, the most comprehensive power of supervision and enforcement with respect to the questions of the reparation. It has to observe the following conditions and determinations:
>
> a) Every part of the entire amount of the determined demands that is not paid in gold, ships, securities or goods or in another way must be secured by Germany under the conditions determined by the Commission through the transfer of a corresponding amount to bonds or obligations of any sort in order to effect an acknowledgement of the owed amount.
>
> b) The Commission will periodically evaluate Germany's payment capacity and examine the German tax system (!), so that, first, all revenues of Germany, including the revenues determined for the interest- and debt servicing of its domestic loans are preferably (!) used for the payment of the sums that it owes under the title or reparations, and secondly, in order to obtain the certainty that the German tax system is exactly (!) as oppressive as that of any other power represented in the Commission.

III. The State

This paragraph is diabolically focussed on the lasting suppression of Germany, it practically contains the possibility, with the reference to some small robber state in which unrestricted taxes are decreed, of simply stipulating the imposition of the same taxes even in Germany. But it also acknowledges at the same time with brutal frankness that even the other nations should be held in the same debt-slavery. And now comes the infamous paragraph c.

In order to facilitate and carry out the restoration of the economic life in the Allied and associated countries, the Commission will, as arranged in Art.232, receive a first payment from Germany as a guarantee and acknowledgement of its guilt, consisting of bonds to the holders, payable in gold, that are free of every tax or charge of any sort (!) that are introduced or can be introduced by the governments of the Reich or of the German states. These bonds are given as instalments (!) and that in three instalments as determined below:

1. 20 billion gold marks are to be paid immediately

2. 40 billion gold marks will be given in bonds that are to bear interest at at an additional charge of 5% + 1% for amortisation from 1926.

    A written obligation to pay 40 billion gold marks more in bonds, with 5% interest as coverage, will be given immediately.

This clause is the core of the entire Versailles dictate . We know that the London Ultimatum[81] not only set fewer payments but, on the contrary, set the entire amount at 132 billion gold marks. Art.16 then declares expressly: "From 1 May, 1921 the German government has to pay for the interests on their debt". The interest rate is set at 5 percent.

Then follows Art.17 which gives a handle to every violation:

Art.17. If Germany should be late in the fulfilment of any debt that the previous section of the treaty lays upon it, the Commission will

---

81   [After the Inter-Allied Reparations Commission had, in January 1921, set the amount that Germany had to pay as reparations at 269 billion gold marks, the British Prime Minister David Lloyd-George presented, on May 5, 1921, a six-day ultimatum to the German ambassador in London, whereby, if Germany did not acknowledge the repayment of 132 billion marks (a somewhat different calculation than the 269 billion of January) as well as the other dictates of the Versailles Treaty, the Allies would occupy the Ruhr region.]

immediately inform every participant power of this default and simultaneously propose the measures to be taken against it.

And now follows one of the most outrageous clauses of the entire treaty:

> Art.18. Germany pledges not to interpret the measures that the Allied and associated powers are justified (and what would not be justified in the eyes of the enemies?) in adopting against an intentional (!) non-compliance of Germany as hostile treatment (!!). These measures could consist of import prohibitions and economic and financial sanctions and in general (!) in all measures (!) that could appear to the concerned governments as demanded by circumstances.

With this clause naturally the door and gate are opened to every, even the most brutal, terror, and the German government has further expressly signed that it may not consider even the greatest oppression, murder of Germans, the most brutal expulsions, plundering, destruction, etc. "as hostile treatment"!

This written delivery of the German people to a cruel, vengeful, implacable enemy is, further, envisaged forever, for Art.23 says:

> The Commission will be dissolved when Germany and its allies have paid all the amounts that it owes for the implementation of the present treaty or according to the decisions of the Commission and when all these amounts or their equivalents are distributed to the participant powers.

This is the eternal interest slavery of Germany.

Perhaps our political friends and enemies will understand now what must be understood by interest slavery, perhaps one will understand why the breaking of this frightful interest slavery stands at the centre of our demands. Perhaps one will understand also why in the case of this demand it is a matter of an international question of the very first order. It is for Germany simply a question of destiny and even for the other nations it is the most decisive question for the recovery.

Compared to this international question, all the other questions sink into nothingness, for without the breaking of interest slavery a rise of productive nations is in general not possible. If the interest slavery

III. The State

now initiated is maintained, the god Mammon would have ascended the throne. God is dead, the souls of the nations die, a human mess fills the world as interest slaves of international finance. Money rules the world.

The regulations of the Versailles dictate were essential points substituted in 1924 by the Dawes Pact. Now after the fears of inflation the further plundering of Germany was to continue "on a more solid foundation". High finance allowed assurances of all sorts to be issued among which the most significant and far-reaching are to be mentioned the denationalisation of the Reichsbank and Reich railways. In spite of all the "silver cloud" prophecies, the German economy continued to collapse, the impossibility of the payments according to the Dawes Pact was finally perceived even by the blindly raging sadists of the implementation. The Young Plan entered in place of the Dawes Pact. It was supposed to bring "alleviations". Now the end has come.

On the horrors of the Dawes Pact Vol.7 of the National Socialist Library (Price 1.80 marks) gives the most precise information, which contains a reprint of the original text along with a comprehensive critical commentary. Vol.13 of the present series deals with the main points of the Young Plan.

The Loan Economy

"If the state needs money, it must borrow this money from those of its citizens who have more of it than they themselves can use. It must naturally pay interest for the return of this money, or else it will not receive the money, it has indeed already enough difficulty in accommodating its loans".

This formulation was used by the former Socialist minister Dr. David[82] with me in a discussion in Berlin. I have placed this formulation here intentionally because it reflects in an exemplary way the interest capitalistic way of thought of our age; that he was of all things a Marxist gives the whole a special attraction.

Now I know from hundreds of discussions and lectures that the above formulation is derived so fully from the present interest capitalistic world of ideas that hardly anybody would feel the falseness of this

---

82 [Eduard David (1863-1930) served as Minister of the Interior in the Weimar Republic from June to October 1919.]

The German State on a National and Socialist Foundation

explanation of the interest- and debt economy of the state, let alone find a correct answer to it.

This has a very simple psychological reason, namely that the above explanation given above applies to the coverage of the monetary need of a private man within the scope of the interest-capitalistic form of the economy.

For the individual private man, as for the private economy in general, the sentence is true: "If anybody needs money, he must borrow this money against interest from those who possess more money than they themselves can use".

But we must indeed avoid answering questions of national financial economy from a private capitalistic viewpoint but from a statesmanly. I mean that it would be indeed a major misfortune if one simply transferred this private economic way of thought unquestioningly to the national economy.

The state with its instruments of power, its sovereign power is indeed not to be equated with any random private man. The state possesses three powerful possibilities through which, by virtue of its sovereignty, it can cover its need for the execution of its tasks. These are its service sovereignty, its coinage sovereignty and its financial sovereignty.

By service sovereignty is to be understood the sovereign right of the state to call on its citizens for free services. This sovereignty of the state over the individual is revealed in its most powerful scope in the compulsory military service and still more in the war service. Faced with the demands that the state can demand of its citizens in war time, all private considerations must step back. Family, profession, business and earnings, everything must be silent when the state calls its sons to the flag. But the state can call its citizens not only to war service, the state can call them even to great economic undertakings, we remember the auxiliary service law that however, unfortunately, quite in contrast to the military service, provided a high and ever increasing payment for the performed services so that soon a deep cleft arose between the front soldiers, who had to offer their lives daily for the fatherland – without payment – and those who were employed, in the homeland, protected behind the front, at a high wage. Just in passing, the strong performances of other nations that were based on service obligations may also be recalled: we recall the building of the Chinese Wall, the circumvallation of our mediaeval cities. Practically

III. The State

therefore it would stand completely within the power sovereignty of the state to revive and expand the old hand- and team- service[83] and to solve large economic tasks with them in this way for the disposal of existing forces.

The coinage sovereignty of the state is a second source of power from which the state can directly cover its money requirement. Nobody contests the state's right to mint coins or to issue treasury notes, indeed beyond that the state has, by virtue of its sovereignty, produced money from every possible source. From copper, nickel, iron, porcelain, aluminium and, above all, from – paper. I need only to recall the time when our Reich government considered it justified to issue daily 100,000,000,000,000 marks and ever more new paper money. We shall not go in greater detail here into the question of whether this was right and acceptable, we have to state here only that the state can actually cover its need by virtue of its coinage sovereignty, and that it is not forced "to borrow money on interest from those of its citizens who have more of it than they themselves can use".

The financial sovereignty or the tax sovereignty of the state will likewise not be able to be contested by anybody, and one who contested this and sought to conduct it practically as an individual would be able to feel the authority of the state in the form of the bailiff. The financial or tax sovereignty of the state, that is, the right of the state to call on its citizens to financial services, is as obvious and as old as state structures. This form is also the most natural and healthy, even though in this field it has been reserved to our times to transform the reasonable sense of taxation into a complete nonsense and to make of the tax system a means for the total plundering of the people in favour of the supranational financial powers. Even here the question of the permissibility of taxes should not occupy us further but only the fact that the state is very well able to cover its money requirement by way of taxes, thus, again, by a way that is not open to the private economy, but which absolutely removes from the state the necessity of coming up with its money requirement through the adoption of an interest payment obligation to the capitalists.

Certainly the state, like every private man, has naturally the further possibility of covering its need by incurring debts. But this is already

---

83 [The farming services, either manual or with animals, demanded of farmers by their lords in the Middle Ages].

The German State on a National and Socialist Foundation

for the private man a two-edged sword; for the state, however, it is, to express it in plain and good German, the stupidest thing that it can in general do. But it is not only the stupidest thing but it is downright criminal with respect to the mission of the state as the protector of the common interests.

The loan economy of the states has virtually ruined the states and delivered them into the hands of international finance, it has delivered the wealth of the nations to the financial powers, and today the state loans are the frightful leech from which the nations are not able to free themselves and through which they will collapse helplessly if we do not determinedly put an end to this spectre through the breaking of interest slavery.

With this we are in the middle of the field of national financial policy, thus in a field in which the normal German does not feel at home at all. What should one do now with all the many and large numbers? The normal state citizen does not in general read budget debates, and he has such a religious respect for the secret paths and misleading ways of the financial art that he would best like to be fully spared of these things. In the unconscious, this certainly is also related to the fact that every individual bears within himself such a slight feeling for the tax sovereignty of the state and nobody wishes to be reminded of numbers. Only when the tax papers fly into his house does the modern man remark that these things actually concern him considerably and that he is always the victim of every sort of false national financial policy.

Now it is extremely remarkable that basically the matters of national financial policy are not at all so opaque and mysterious as they appear at first glance, indeed that they are basically so clear and simple that they can be grasped by every average understanding at least in their broad outlines.

It therefore requires no great constitutional explanations that the state very well possesses the described possibilities to cover its money requirement, for everybody knows and has experienced in his own life what the nature of the service sovereignty of the state is, and everybody receives in his hand daily the paper notes issued by the state, and nobody is spared the tax. It would therefore be the most natural thing in the world if the state covered its money requirement exclusively in these three ways.

III. The State

For the private man however these three ways are not open, for neither could he call on his neighbour successfully to work- or tax service nor would he be secure if he attempted to print money on his own and bring it into circulation. For him there is indeed only the way of incurring debt on interest, if he already absolutely thinks that he is able to become happy only with others' monies and cannot avoid incurring debts.

But that the state in general sees as right the sole means of accepting interest-bearing loans – thus debts, when it needs money and applies its other sovereign rights today only in an underhand manner to collect the incurred debts from the people, these are conditions for which one seeks in vain for a reasonable explanation. There is indeed no reasonable explanation for it, but only the fact that our entire thought even in national financial political matters is directed or corrupted in a private capitalistic manner. With such a general pollution of public opinion, such apparently logical explanations for the loan policy of the state as I have reported play a great, indeed an all-important role.

The Jew has proved himself to be a master of psychagogy even in these matters. It is, in such cases, always very hard not to speak at once generally of direct corruption of the responsible statesmen, the presumption is obvious, and yet in most cases there has been no corruption but only uncertainty in matters of the financial and credit system, short-sightedness and complacency that have led to the fact that the state financial administrations have fallen slowly but surely into a loan delirium from which they up to now see no exit.

To this development of the circumstances has contributed in a very essential manner the fact that one at first considered the financing of large public works like railway building, etc., which promised to yield a revenue, through loans as harmless. One decided in the following manner: From the revenues of the railways or waterways the interest can be immediately covered, then we indeed have the pricing under control. With its own resources the state cannot draw such large works at one stroke from its treasury, so it thankfully accepts the offered credit help of the banks. This removes the trouble from the government of approving new taxes in the state parliament, the liquid resources of the state are not claimed, and the railways can easily pay the interests from the surpluses. The seductive arts of loan capital, which in itself can do nothing with money if it does not find

The German State on a National and Socialist Foundation

anybody who takes it away from it and pays it interest in addition, succeeded in turning black into white and in making the state itself an interest collector for private capital.

Even the simplest economic reflection on the part of a government or a parliament conscious of its responsibility however should have led to the following: If one builds the railways with foreign money and one must pay for it, year in year out, only 5% interest, with everything connected with it, one pays back in 20 years already the entire amount once, in 40 years already twice and yet the same debt remains outstanding. These extraordinary amounts which exceed many times the initial investment costs must indeed be raised once again indirectly from the people, the entire population, who must pay the railway transport tariffs raised precisely according to these interest amounts. A one-time announcement to the people of a large railway levy is, or would have been, better. Then these levies would, of course, have been rather oppressive for some years but also for not much longer, as the the transport costs and the railways would have very soon become a really debt-free asset of the state which would have later assured it large yearly revenues. But it is the old story that one would rather cut off the dog's tail bit by bit because one thinks it would be so much less painful for it. Naturally, the opposite is true. The investment costs of such a national undertaking must indeed be paid by the population, but if they are developed on loans, then there inevitably enter, in addition, the interests that amount in the course of the years to many times the debt itself. It is therefore a sheer financial stupidity to finance such public works through loans. Already here we may point to that which will rescue the state from its loan madness: nobody can forbid the state, for example for such productive undertakings, to issue credit notes, state treasury credit notes, and pay for the works thereby. Such a creation of money of the state in cases where there can be no question of an inflation at all, because there is a new value also for the new tokens, would resolve at one stroke all the difficulties and free the state and the people forever from the interest-bearing debt to private capital.

We shall have to go into greater detail into this problem in another place. A skilled financial administration should be able to arrange things in such a way that such large works are carried out from special taxes along with the use of other revenue sources of the state and only with a partial issue of new notes. This possibility would of course occur to a considerable extent only if all other state expenditures, especially the so-called unproductive ones for administration, administration

III. The State

of justice, education, etc., could be covered from the surpluses of the state's commercial enterprises.

This may, in view of the present frantic deficit economy of the railways, post, etc., sound like an irony and yet we were not so far from such possibilities, as I already showed in 1919 in my first publication in the Süddeutsche Monatshefte (February), "What now?" under the heading "The radical means". Only the interest obligation of the state to private capital separated us from this ideal condition of a national financial economy. The delusion already effective at that time, that the state, when it needs money, must simply pump money into itself at interest, has prevented this.

It is clear, and everybody should have been able to follow my explanations, that the state is in no way directed to foreign money, thus to the incurring of debt, when it wishes to undertake something, that it, for example, could demand work- and team-service and that it finally would be doubtless justified in issuing state treasury credit notes for such goals, in order to institute these works with them without a burdening of the people. Such a procedure would have the enormous advantage of freeing such works from the start from every interest- and toll-obligation; the works would become immediately free and debt-free state property. From the revenues of the works the issued state treasury vouchers could indeed be redeemed and destroyed in a short time; the products of such works, or the freight- and passenger transport prices, could be reduced quite considerably. Thereby the greatest services could in general be rendered to the entire national economy, the state could have obtained quite significant revenue sources which would have been of the greatest use to the entire national community and would also have made the state itself quite independent of high finance. But it also should have been so. For the state is the master of the financial system and not high finance, that is, it will be so in the National Socialist state of the future.

It has been really a psychagogic fraudulent trick that the banks have succeeded in not allowing such obvious and self-evident thought-processes which – once expressed – are no longer to be contradicted, and in befuddling the state and economy with the sentence cited above and roping them into the interest slavery to capital.

I know that, even though these things are now clear as daylight, still many of my readers mistrust their healthy human understanding and simply do not wish to believe how such an absurdity could have been possible and would rather suppose: "That cannot be right, our statesmen cannot have been so stupid – but I just cannot judge this". This confession to a lack of judgement with regard to such a plain state incompetence in financial political matters stands doubly in contradiction to the otherwise ready fault-finding and ranting on state measures and to the fact that it is a question here of matters that hit every individual most keenly in his wallet

To these people I would like to leave another viewpoint for consideration which is related to the method of credit approval through the provincial or Reich parliament.

Such large state tasks are indeed deliberated thoroughly in the parliaments. After long debates the credits are finally "approved". The average state-citizen believes now that now everything is in order and that the state, which is indeed such a rich and powerful guy, already possesses the approved millions. Quite clever persons will perhaps still scratch behind their ear and say to themselves, 'That means new taxes again'. But I think I may boldly maintain that, apart from the initiated – to whom neither the representatives nor the ministers need to belong –, indeed perhaps only one at most becomes clear of the fact that this large credit approval in the provincial or Reich parliament signifies nothing but the permission to have this "credit" loaned to itself at interest in another way. This "credit approval through parliament" thus empowers only the concerned minister to get this credit at interest at the large banks. In this way the "credit approval through parliament" naturally becomes a farce, a comedy, for the entire population - which must in the final analysis pay for capital and interest - was not in a position also to really supply the "credit", no, it must first be created by large loan capital.

The only logical and natural thing would indeed be that, in the case of a credit approval through the parliament, simultaneously and automatically there would also be an approval that now the state bank would also pay out or authorise the approved sums on the basis of payment orders from the implementing authorities to the concerned entrepreneurs.

The credits are approved, for the necessary currency something must be done; it is therefore senseless if – as is now common – first a loan must be written out and then the just "approved" credits are in a way given a second time by the capitalists.

III. The State

Now one may be able to maintain that surplus money from the state is drawn just in this way and that this must have a beneficial influence on the general financial situation of the country, that thus such a credit management will operate in an inflation-reducing manner. But this is naturally in no way the case and indeed for reasons that cannot be contested by any banking expert. It may be admitted that a quite smaller part of such drafts and payments of such loans is paid in cash, it is a question here of the circle of small savers who find their way to the bank with such drafts, who have saved a pair of hundred or thousand marks that they would now like to invest in an interest certificate, in such a magic paper from which one needs to cut out only a piece every year in order to be paid out a certain amount without the certificate becoming less valuable thereby. But the monies entering the bank in this way are quite negligible. In addition, the banks at which such monies are deposited for their part do not at all convey these cash amounts to the state treasury but the transfer of such draft amounts is conducted exclusively by way of transfer or clearance.

But all larger drafts on such loans are conducted by the capitalists already from the start, in their banks, by way of transfer without cash or through the process of banking transactions, etc.

In reality therefore no cash comes into the hands of the state and, if it receives such, it must immediately give it away for the execution of its works. This supposed advantage therefore does not exist. On the contrary this follows: The state, as we know, issues for loaned amounts so-called security certificates or bonds. These bonds of the state are finely, or not so finely, printed papers which contain a debt instrument endowed with all state safeguards on the received amounts, and in addition the necessary determinations of the interest payment dates and, on their own coupon-sheets, the coupons on the basis of which the state pledges to pay quarter-yearly, half-yearly or annually the interests for the amounts noted in the coupon-sheet. Besides, to this coupon-sheet is added another so-called renewal certificate (talon) which entitles the owner to the receipt of a new coupon-sheet if the first has expired after a certain number of years.

Now such a security certificate that is issued by the state for which the state is liable with its entire wealth for capital and interest means certainly purchasing capacity in the hand of the owner. The owner of such state certificates can indeed buy something for himself with these certificates at any time, whether he gives these certificates

The German State on a National and Socialist Foundation

directly as payment or he first sells these certificates at the stock-exchange or his banker and then pays cash with the proceeds.

Now there is no doubt at all that the issue of new security certificates by the state means the creation of additional purchasing capacity – whether this is right or justified does not interest us here at the moment -, quite the same would occur if, for example, the state printed new paper money. The difference would consist in the fact that in one case security certificates are produced which burden the state, apart from the debt, with a lasting interest obligation, whereas in the case of the new issue of paper money an interest-obligation does not at all come into consideration. We see therefore already now that the last form in any case would be the more favourable for the state and the people.

But now, if we follow the method of such financings further, it emerges that a direct financing of large state works with an avoidance of the loan route reveals further huge advantages.

We have seen that the currently adopted form of the financing of state works leads to the creation of additional purchasing capacity, which is represented by the issue of new security certificates. In this case naturally the entire new loan amounts will and must be given out all at once, even if the railways, waterways, etc. to be built newly are only in a construction stage and still do not represent any real value worth mentioning.

If one moves to financing such large state works in the way proposed by me, then the enormous advertising costs for the loan first disappear. One may remember what enormous amounts are devoured by the tenders in the newspapers alone. Further the percentages that are granted to the banks and other credit institutions from the start disappear. Even these are, again, millions. Further, one tends to issue the loans under the par value, in other words, for a 1000 mark bond only 970 marks more or less are to be paid by the purchaser of these certificates, and yet he receives the full amount with interest. Even these are losses that from the start become burdens to the state or the enterprise and in favour of the capitalist. Indeed one tends "to decorate" such loans with other attractions, as the stock-exchange expression goes, by holding out in prospect special extra benefits which may even include a tax exemption. I recall here the mining premium loan that displayed the most fantastic of such attractions that a state ever stooped to. The lottery- and gambling devil was set in the service of the loan advertisement in that one promised to

III. The State

pay out winnings of millions on a very large number of 1000 mark bonds; besides, so-called bonus payments were held out, and further, an announced interest-rate at 5% that was however hedged in with clauses, and, in addition, in the case of a series of taxes the savings premium loan was exempt from every tax! From where one wished to obtain the enormous amounts to pay these premiums and benefits, these fabulous lottery winnings, nobody considered – even though it had to be clear to every serious and perceptive man that all these amounts would have to be drawn out once again from the pockets of the people. For, the amounts received then were immediately used for the most urgent expenditures. These are all financial political crimes against the people in which one must only wonder at the consummate insolence with which they are staged.

If one therefore does not at all take the loan route, but directly the way of direct money creation, then all these hard and unjust burdens of the state budget would be removed – one would not even have to raise the necessary amounts all at once in new paper money but this could take place quite slowly, according as even the new works proceed. This would have the further enormous advantage that there could be no question of the issue of uncovered money, for new money will be given only when another considerable section of the works has been completed. We would have to do here with a money fully covered through real values, thus with a money that is stable, with a money that is matched by so many hours of performed work. But even this form of a successive issue of new money for construction which already appears much more favourable is not in any way the final step. For it will not at all be proved necessary to bring an amount of money equivalent to the newly created works into circulation, for the newly issued notes indeed flow back again into the public state treasuries; they can thus be issued once again without new series having to be brought into circulation. And now let us go a step further, that is, let us declare the issue of one's own new money for such special state tasks as being in itself fundamentally not at all necessary, even if we could very well explain the permissibility, and also especially the clarity, of the financing process in the issue of one's own money for construction and wished to adhere to it for certain purposes.

This last step is the complete cashless financing of such state tasks. It is, as have already shown above, erroneous to assume that the state would, through the loan, come into cash with which it could pay the entrepreneur and workers of railway or electricity plant constructions. Nevertheless, the entrepreneurs will have to draw out weekly from their banks the necessary amounts for the payment of their work in cash. The banks for their part must cover these extraordinarily large demands on their treasury stocks once again from the central banks or the Reichsbank, etc. Now, in normal times, the entire existing liquidity already suffices fully for the weekly wage payments of the entire workforce, and it is fundamentally a matter of indifference if temporarily, for example, larger workforces are concentrated in one place in the construction of the Bavarian Walchensee power plant, for, if they were not employed there, they would even when distributed in other enterprises have to expect and receive their weekly wage payments, or receive money by means of unemployment insurance. That means that it is a quite general state task to take care of the total need of means of payment for the entire national economy, no matter whether greater workforces are temporarily employed in one place for the execution of large state works or not.

The provision of means of payment for the wage payments and the implementation of the other cashless transfers to the entrepreneurs are tasks of payment transactions and have nothing at all to do causally with the credit situation.

It would therefore be the most obvious and natural thing if with the credit approval for some large state work through the lawful representation of the entire population were bound, at the same time, the authorisation that the state bank may, on the basis of these approved credits, carry out the necessary payments. Obviously in the normal way - that these payments are made only when the different contracted state authorities (agricultural departments, street and river engineering departments, railway construction sections, special departments for special purposes, etc.) have examined the payment amounts demanded by the entrepreneurs and, in accordance with the regulations and the contract, authorised payment.

The entire loan swindle that is thrown in – for it is nothing but the modern form of cheating a nation – is completely useless and only harmful.

The Reichsbank Corporation

The Reichsbank is not, as every credulous state-citizen may after all believe, really a state bank but a stock company. The Reichsbank is thus in no way a state institution even if the state had, up to June 1922, when it was fully "autonomised" on the demands of the Entente, certain

III. The State

regulatory rights. Even the officials of the bank were named and paid by the Reich, but the advisory council was composed exclusively of representatives of the world of big banks and of international Jewry – the two are the same circle of people.

Already in its foundation in 1873 the first advisory council recorded among around 15 members the following names: Baron Rothschild, Privy Councillor of Commerce Bleichröder, Privy Councillor of Commerce Mendelssohn, Theodor Plaut, Privy Councillor of Commerce Oppenheimer, Privy Councillor of Commerce Warschauer and Privy Councillor of Commerce Zwicker, Councillor of Commerce Stern, Councillor of Commerce Gelpke; so eleven pure-bred big Jews and, as decoration, four more gentlemen with German names.

It was again a clever chess-move with which the banker advising Bismarck, Bleichröder, recommended to the old Reichschancellor that the Reichsbank be developed not as a pure state institution because thereby it would not be able to be appropriated by the enemy in case of war on the basis of the internationall recognised security of private property, whereas as a pure state bank it would stand immediately open to the attack of the enemy.

In reality, the clever Jew, along with the other big financiers, naturally wished only to get the principal financial institute of the Reich into his sphere of power. The gentlemen succeeded in this too and the Reich therewith totally renounced one of the most important fields of its coinage sovereignty – its right of issuing banknotes.

The Reichsbank occupies today a quite special position in the financial system of the German Reich, a position about which the least important people are clear even today regarding its frightful consequences for the state and the people.

It must be the task of an individual investigation to precisely examine in what way the big banks have misused their decisive influence on the Reichsbank, since its foundation, to their egoistic ends.

So long as Bismarck was in office his statesmanly view and the respect for him kept the stock-exchange hyenas under control; only once in the entire history of the Reichsbank did Bismarck make use of the chancellor's veto provided for in the Reichsbank law, namely when he forbade the acceptance of Russian stocks. Today the Reichsbank has, under the friendly pressure of the international bankers, as already mentioned at the start, been made fully independent. The Reichsgovernment thus has no further possibility of acting in a decisive way on the conduct of the business.

The interest slavery of the nations means the rule of the bank and stock-exchange. The breaking of interest slavery is by far the greatest task of National Socialism.

Everything that happens today in the state and economy – everything becomes a demand for interest of large capital against productive work. If a railway is built, there results a loan therefrom, if a war is conducted, war loans result therefrom, if natural resources or hydro-energy are developed, there result hydro-energy loans therefrom, if a factory is expanded, new shares are issued, if a new enterprise is founded, some interest capitalistic company form is chosen that allows the work and the risk to flow to the entrepreneurs and the lion's share of the profits to the financiers. If it does not proceed any more by way of loans, the far simpler and more extensive way of money-printing is chosen, as in the time of the inflation of 1923, which likewise gathers in the greatest interests for large capital. As in the case of King Midas in the saga, for whom everything that he touched turned into gold, so today everything that happens turns into interest-bearing securities.

Unfortunately the world-bankers have a damned good appetite and securities are indeed their favourite food, which obviously suits them excellently. We cannot count on their going hungry, like King Midas, for whom, as is well-known, even the food in his mouth turned to gold. On the contrary, the workers will first go hungry before the interest lords will.

They also do not at all think of giving up or softening their rule, so this interest rule must be broken.

Now we have to illuminate a third aspect that will complete and round off the picture of the interest capitalistic exploitation even for the layman, that is inflation.

Inflation

Inflation is the clearly visible expression of our financial political misery. Inflation affects everybody – everybody who must earn his livelihood - with frightful severity.

III. The State

But from whence does inflation come? To this question one can hear a large number of explanations which are partly taken from the narrow viewpoint of the person answering, partly from the dictionary of demagogic slogans, and partly indicate actual partial causes without however correctly hitting the ultimate motivating cause. When one hears these causes of inflation identified by the different parties, there is soon no social order and no profession any more that would not be designated by some side as the cause of inflation.

For those who have followed the explanations of the book on interest slavery[84] the answer is not hard to find. The original guilt for inflation is borne by the interest obligation of work to capital.

Interest – tax – inflation, thus does the logical chain run which, starting from the disastrous and absurd promise of interest on the part of the state, forces the consequence that the state must extract the accepted interest obligations from the people through taxes; the taxes, and indeed taxes of all kinds, direct and indirect, duties, as well as the most objectionable indirect taxes, those of the uncovered banknote issue, then drag in inflation along with them. In this way it continues in an eternal cycle, for the inflation conditions ever greater expenses of the state which it, trapped in the loan madness, always thinks that it can cover only through the acceptance of new debts, these new debts bear new interests in themselves, the new interests make new taxes necessary, the tax legislation gradually fails completely, for, in the case of such currency collapses, all the tax revenues remain far behind the currency devaluation and now the state surrenders without resistance to the financial Bolshevism of the money printing press, as we have horribly experienced in the inflation of 1923.

My first polemical works were primarily dedicated to the uncovering of these connections. In the Manifesto for the breaking of interest slavery I developed in broad outlines generally the all-overarching significance of the interest problem, in the State bankruptcy: The solution I quite specifically revealed the stupidity of the state loan system and pointed to the innumerable tax laws which made more expensive the livelihood of the broad masses, whose productions had to be used completely for the interest service. In the work The coming tax strike, with the new flood of tax laws from 1920 and 1921,

---

84   Feder's *Manifest zur Brechung der Zinsknechtschaft des Geldes* was first published in 1919. See my translation of this work, *Manifesto For Breaking The Financial Slavery To Interest*, London: Black House Publishing, 2015.

as well the Reichsbudget for 1918, the conclusive proof was offered that the entire financial administration of the Reich and the states is completely yoked to the interest service for large loan capital. In the last book, however, the way is already indicated to a reversal of these completely squalid circumstances with a quite palpable example.

It is quite obvious that, through the flooding of a national economy with paper money, the purchasing power of this paper money must steadily go down.

Since money in its innermost character, as we have recognised, is a token of performed work, the so-called quantity theory of money, at least in its essential features, must be acknowledged by us. This theory teaches that the amount of money found in circulation in a national economy must remain in a certain stable relationship if changes in purchasing power are not to emerge. The money stands to a certain extent against stocks of goods and – calculated from the amount of goods – a certain number of units of value of the customary currency is produced, that is, the average price of the goods. Here I stress very strongly the adjective 'average'. Indeed, one must go farther and say: the average price level – thus in no way the amount of the individual prices – stands in a certain dependency on the amount of the purchasing power present in total in the country. But purchasing power is already a much more comprehensive concept than only the amount of cash assets. But we do not wish to get lost here very much in economic details, for otherwise the question of effective and potential purchasing power in its effect on the prices must be broached here.[85] Anyway it is certain that, for example, a multiplication thousand times of the circulating currency must naturally bring with it a multiplication roughly thousand times of the prices. In reality it is not the prices that have really risen, the purchasing power of the mark has just diminished in inverse relation to the multiplication of the amount of the currency.

---

85 Potential purchasing power is the saved purchasing power that does not at the moment weigh on the market. To this belongs hoarded cash as well the firmly invested savings capital.

Effective purchasing power is the total amount of all demand claims on the national economy which in the form of cash or in the form of securities are applied to the goods market and seek to transform themselves into material goods.

Potential purchasing power can be transformed at any time into effective, in the case of this phenomenon one speaks of the "flight from the mark".

III. The State

The basic cause of inflation is – the interest obligation of the state. This interest obligation makes taxes necessary, for the state can only give what it must again extract in some form from its citizens.

This form of robbery of its citizens by the state is, as we have seen, a threefold one – either through direct taxes or in more effective form through indirect taxes or in the special indirect form of inflation. The last form is the most objectionable, it is also that with which bankrupt states seek to hold their head above water – it is the most perfect counterfeiting. But this last form is especially so harmful because thereby the savings wealth of the most efficient and industrious part of the population is simply destroyed.

This is one of the most shocking chapters in the tragedy of the German people. Hundred thousands of industrious manual labourers, employees, officials, members of free professions, doctors, engineers, etc. have all their life long, through tenacious tireless work, saved for themselves and for their families so that they could enjoy an old age free of care and independent. They have collected their savings penny by penny and mark by mark, and every mark means the guarantee of the subsistence minimum for every day in old age. But the state, to which these unfortunate people have entrusted their savings, did not, in the inflation of 1923, pay in any way for a mark which had been entrusted to it in some way as savings – even not when these saved pennies had been deposited at that time in shiny gold pieces – about 30 million papiermarks,[86] but it availed itself of the decline of the currency caused by itself and said: a mark = a mark. Therewith it robbed all these men of the fruits of their lifelong work and pushed them into the most bitter distress. They were then fobbed off by the state with pathetic and miserable handouts, private charity had to step in with help – but precisely this form was especially shameful for those affected, for from the private hands these gifts remained actual handouts, charitable gifts for which these unfortunate people had to be thankful, even though it was a matter of organised robbery of well earned rights. Of rights which, if they were restored, would not even make a "thanks" from the robbed necessary.

---

86 [The papiermark was established in August 1914 on account of the fall of the mark, and the connection between the goldmark and gold was abandoned. The rate of inflation continued to rise until November 1923, when the currency was stabilised through the announcement of the creation of a new rentenmark valued at 1 trillion papiermarks. The rentenmark, which came into effect in 1924, was itself replaced later in the same year by the Reichsmark.]

The German State on a National and Socialist Foundation

We have already pointed in other passages to the fact that a false principle avenged itself frightfully on these poor people – indeed the ideal of capital pension. Not as if these circles had deserved this fate, on the contrary – it will be an honourable duty of the National State to compensate these robbed people as well as possible. Yet, it remains to be hoped that this frightful lesson will nevertheless continue to vibrate in the unconscious of the people and that the capital pension ideal will sink and will help the right savings ideal – the purely German idea of old age care, care of women and children through the creation of a home of their own, field and garden, etc. - to a breakthrough and victory.

The second form of robbery of the citizens by the state mentioned above is the indirect tax. Indirect tax is, in its consequences, indeed a social crime. Ruthlessly and relentlessly, in a form that nobody can avoid, it hits the great mass of the population with total severity, whereas the rich are in general hardly touched by the indirect taxes.

The direct tax is, if it is graded according to the economic performance capacity of the tax-payer, in itself a just and right tax. A direct tax is also, as a contributory payment to the state for communal tasks, in no way a tax which must essentially make the production more expensive, for it should be taken only where actual surpluses beyond the coverage of the adequate life-necessities are present. But as direct tax is treated today, it, like inflation, amounts to a sheer robbery and places itself in direct contradiction to the guarantee of property expressed in Art.153 of the Weimar constitution.

In summary, let it be once again pointed out that we have to do here with an inflation which operates generally as a consequence of the interest obligation of the state to international finance. It is a matter here of a lasting blood-sucking from the economic body of our nation in favour of the supranational financial power for which our own state acts as a tax-collector.

It is a matter here of a quite special form of inflation – the interest capitalistic inflation. Natural inflation arises when insufficient harvest or an epidemic hits the country, when the natural demands are greater than the existing supply. Such an inflation is however always only of a temporary nature. The next fertile year removes the distress and the prices return to their natural level.

The interest capitalistic inflation however is like a devouring fire which is not extinguished until it has consumed all the treasures of the world and made the whole of mankind interest-slaves of international finance – or until the interest slavery is broken.

National Financial Reform

After such a thorough diagnosis of the illness of our state finances, as of our financial system in general, we may hope to be able to give the right prescriptions for the remedy.

Those regulations and measures that regulate the transition from the present situation to the future form do not belong within the scope of this work. For these measures is valid the general guideline that through these where possible every disturbance of the economic life must be avoided. Naturally it will not happen without a certain severity here and there and without temporary interventions but, even in the case of a most carefully prepared operation, it does not happen without a certain small loss of blood.

Our great shining final goal is the breaking of the interest slavery.

The first and fundamental measure, which results from the surrender of the national financial system to a private institution, the Reichsbank, plc, is the nationalisation of the Reichsbank.

It must already be quite obvious from the scope of this bank that a "Reichsbank" has indeed to be an institution of the Reich, just as the Reichspost or the Reichscourt. It must be absolutely declared as a misleading of public opinion that the Reichsbank, plc, is allowed to bear this name.

The task of a real Reichsbank must correspondingly be a two-fold one. First, the provision of financial businesses of the Reich must lie with it, insofar as these cannot be provided for by individual administrative positions themselves and directly, as this is indeed the case with the post and the railways, and, secondly, it must form the strong backing for the entire national economy in the fiduciary mediation of payment transactions. Its task must, further, be to see to it that constantly sufficient cash assets are present for monetary transactions. For this range of tasks it must be the executive organ of the national financial administration, which must be placed fully under it. The officials of the Reichsbank must be state officials, like the other officials as well. An advisory council, which is constituted of representatives of big Jewry, as that of today, is naturally completely superfluous. It is indeed sufficient if a special state commissioner for the supervision of the financial conduct of the bank, who is responsible for the financial conduct of the bank, is appointed by the state. The tasks of the bank will be precisely circumscribed by its own Reichsbank law so that already the financial conduct of the bank would provide a guarantee that the institution of the Reichsbank serves only the national interests.

But we have now already a banking institution which corresponds completely to these demands that we must place upon the Reichsbank. This is the Bavarian State Bank. The Bavarian State Bank is actually a purely national bank, and nobody will be able to maintain that it has not fulfilled its tasks as a banking institution in an unobjectionable way. This naturally with the caveat that it has likewise worked according to the general customs of the interest capitalistic economy. But in any case this bank has served the monetary transactions without considering profitability for the bank capital as the first task. It has thereby manifested the following very remarkable phenomenon that the bank, with its own extremely small capital of only 8,000,000 marks, was very well in a position to serve all the demands of monetary transactions and to manage revenues of billions.

It is not uninteresting to state that, in the Stock-exchange Yearbook (Saling's Stock-exchange Yearbook, A Handbook for capitalists and stockholders, for 1914/15, presented by the German Bank), the existence of this Bavarian State Bank (at that time still "Royal Bavarian Bank") is simply ignored, even though there were opportunity and place to mention it on page 644 of this handbook of this nevertheless significant state institution. But a bank which does not exclusively serve private capitalistic aims is clearly, for high finance, not a bank.

It is further remarkable that, immediately after the war and the Munich Bolshevist period, efforts were under way to place the Bavarian State Bank "on a broader basis", as the delightful stock-exchange technical expression for it ran, in order to make even this independent institution available for the "making profitable" of private capital. Our demand thus has a practically preserved model in the Bavarian State Bank. The objection that it is not possible to conduct a bank as a state institution is thereby refuted.

For the Reichsbank itself, the Reichsbank law in fact proposed a nationalisation according to which the Reich would have the right, after a year's notice, for the first time on 1.1.1891, then in periods of ten

III. The State

years, either to abolish the Reichsbank and to acquire the assets of the same (including the enormously valuable buildings) against a payment of the net asset value (!) or to acquire all the shares at face value (!!). On 1 January 1921 thus the Reich would have been able to make good a serious mistake of the Reichslegislation against the German people if it acquired the entire property of the Reichsbank for the trifle of 180 million – that is the face value of the Reichsbank shares.

The *Völkische Beobachter*,[87] which was at that time not yet in the possession of the National Socialist German Workers' Party, which however was at that time already led by men who belonged to the intellectual precursors of National Socialism, and the weekly of Dr. Sch. Pudor, *Der deutsche Finanzmann*,[88] pointed this out in time – of course as the only public German newspaper voices – naturally without any success.

It is further remarkable that, although the Reichsbank shares are made out to names, not less than 2153 foreigners were in the possession of Reichsbank shares! What part of the entire capital of the Reichsbank these 2153 foreigners (as of 1913) disposed of is unfortunately not apparent from the Reichsbank disclosures. In any case, it is a matter of a very considerable percentage after the number of local share-holders is given at only 16,646. Now it is clear that, in the case of the local share-holders, very much smaller amounts may have been acquired, whereas naturally it may be rightly assumed that a foreigner, when he buys German Reichsbank shares, does not acquire only one or two pieces, but straightaway a neat package. This fact hides the incredible situation that quite significant sums were drawn away in the form of dividends, even during the war, from the "German Reichsbank" to foreign countries.

Now, the profit sharing of the Reichsbank, which derives its main profits from bill discounting – as we have learnt above –, is a most highly original one. First, the share-holders receive a preference dividend of 3½%, and from the remaining profit then a quarter is distributed to the share-holders. Three-fourths of this remaining profit are transferred to the Reich, after a further 10% is transferred to a reserve fund. In 1913, 31,025,555 marks were transferred in this way to the Reich. For that reason the Reich has conferred on this remarkable institution the so-called bank-note printing privilege, that is, the right

---

87   [See above p.20n]
88   [See above p.9.]

The German State on a National and Socialist Foundation

to issue bank-notes according to the need of its transactions. Up to the breakout of the war, the Reichsbank was at least supposed to keep ready, as a cover for these bank-notes, up to a third of gold or silver in German or foreign coins or in bars. After even this restriction fell, there stood no more obstacle in the way of the limitless paper money printing. The only coverage (!) which the Reichsbank had for its paper money was the wonderful Reichstreasury bills – thus once again only another paper, behind which stood a bankrupt state. No wonder if, amidst such conditions, an unstoppable collapse of the German currency had to occur.

It is doubtless a quite important state task for a nationalised bank to always take care that the claims of the economy for means of payment are fully satisfied; for only if no deadlocks occur here, even if the other financial institutions can satisfy all claims fully, is an interest extortion on the basis of money shortage - which can rise to the greatest world crises - excluded. Conversely, the issued amounts of money flow back, even in times of a lesser buoyancy of the economy, to the Reichsbank through the innumerable channels of public money transactions so that it can draw the notes again from the circulation. In the case of the Bank of England, it is customary, as is well-known, that a note which flows back to the bank is not given out again but is exchanged for a new one while the old one is destroyed. This happens primarily for hygienic reasons.

Now the question of the currency will in the future indeed be of increasing significance after the so-called money surrogates, like bills of exchange and cheques, and especially the cashless money transactions, gain increasing importance.

In such a clearing economy, the postal cheque offices, which already today are exemplary for pure monetary transactions on a cashless and interest-free basis, will gain extraordinarily in significance. In the present-day postal cheque offices are to be glimpsed the core cells that are easily to be developed for an ideal monetary transaction system under state supervision – completely corresponding to the national passenger- and goods transport.

Nobody can contest that the payment transactions through the postal cheque offices are handled more quickly and reliably. It hardly matters that credit- and debit notes are not dealt with within 48 hours at most, when, on the other hand, one can experience with the banks today that credit notes for amounts long received are produced only 8 to 14 days

III. The State

later. If the bank customer needs money for his enterprise, he is still forced to claim bank credit. In the case of the monetary transaction through the postal cheque offices the entire interest calculation is removed. This means a quite enormous relief and simplification of the payment transaction and especially at the end-of-year deadlines. The postal cheque customer receives on 2 January every year - as also every day on demand - the exact information on the condition of his account in the postal cheque account.

The mediation of the monetary transaction through the banks is thus in no way especially advantageous for the economy. The pure monetary transaction through the banks burdens the production only with provisions of all sorts, and only and exclusively the banks have a benefit from the interests but never the one who makes use of the bank. For the just factory owner and entrepreneur the receipt of a couple of marks interest for temporary credits is not at all important. A just entrepreneur directs himself in such a way that he has disposable in the bank only so much money that he can defray the wages and other current payments therefrom.

The postal cheque accounts correspond to these demands completely and it is not by chance that, even during the war, the English society of "Fabians", the "Fabian Society",[89] in London directed a memorandum to the Lord Chancellor of the Exchequer with the title: "How do we pay for the war?", in which they pointed to the organisation of the German and Austrian postal cheque accounts as a support. Enemies are always sharp-sighted and when they indicate an institution for their own country as exemplary then one can be certain that there is something in it.

The same thing that was said about the nationalisation of the Reichsbank is true naturally also of the nationalisation of the other central banks, for Bavaria, thus, of the "Bavarian Central Bank". The Bavarian Central Bank is likewise a pure stock company, in which a majority of the share-holders, for example, can simply decide to distribute the gold reserves of the bank, on which the bank's privilege of issuing notes lies, to the share-holders. Indeed we still

---

89 [The Fabian Society is a democratic socialist organisation that favours reform rather than revolution. It was founded in 1884 and its early members included George Bernard Shaw, H.G. Wells, Annie Besant, Leonard and Virginia Woolf, though the most significant of these were Sidney and Beatrice Webb. It was Sidney Webb indeed who composed the constitution of the nascent Labour Party in 1900.]

The German State on a National and Socialist Foundation

remember that attempts in this direction were made by the Jewish banker Schweißheimer in Munich. This time the plan foundered on the objection of the Bavarian government. The Bavarian state had acquired at that time a sixth of the shares while a further sixth had been acquired by the Bavarian Mortgage and Discount Bank and the remaining two thirds were given out to the share-holders.

It is in itself absolutely monstrous that a state must fear that the gold stock of the central bank could be endangered by the intervention of the "share-holders" of this bank. One who knows the Jewish tenacity knows that the danger for Bavaria for its gold stock was nowhere near removed by the fact that the government for once remained firm. Against this there is indeed only the one radical means of the nationalisation of the central banks. Apart from the Bavarian Central Bank, we have in Germany also the Baden Bank, the Saxon Bank in Dresden and the Württemberg Central Bank.

In the case of the nationalisation of the Reichsbank and the central banks, the officials and employees of the banks will obviously be taken over in the same capacity by the state as state servants. The right to issue notes will thereby be exercised exclusively by the state. Such an issue of notes can occur only after an ordinance of the Ministry of Finance and only against complete coverage. Here in this connection is to be resolved the great task of the stabilisation of our currency. This is however not a task within the smaller circle of central banks; they only have to take care that no issue of notes takes place without coverage.

For the production of notes the determinations up to now are valid. Every imitation will be punished with the greatest strictness according to the prescriptions of the penal code, Section VIII, Arts.146-152.

The shareholders will be compensated. Any claim to the gold stocks of the bank on the part of the share-holders will be legally excluded.

A real stabilisation of our currency is fully excluded so long as one expects, in the way described, interest and duty charges of the German people that cannot in the long run be fulfilled. It is also false to want to maintain a radical means for a stabilisation of the currency. It is a matter here not of a special problem that one could separate from the international problem of the interest economy. So long as this international robber economy of the all-Jewish high finance continues to exist, the currencies of the different nations will always

III. The State

remain the welcome object of speculation of high finance. Further, the stability of a currency – thus that which the inner meaning of the term "currency" expresses - depends on other factors, above all on the activity or passivity of the balance of trade. Here our glance is extended beyond the limits of our fatherland, and the home economy enters into mutual relations with the national economies of foreign countries.

In order to quickly find one's bearings in this enormous field of international finance we must likewise have in mind once again that the meaning and goal of this international economy is not the profitability for private capital, but the covering of need. Everything else is only an accessory, an aid. The international financial economy - the international payment transactions - is however today that which appears as the principal thing and which today actually plays the chief role. It is the international banking houses that today actually rule the world, which "cover" the monetary need of the states, and have therefore arrogated the rule to themselves; it is the international banking houses that today control production in gigantic trusts, iron, steel, petroleum, canned food, grain, fat, oil, cotton, etc. The international banking houses financed the wars, the large banking houses financed and controlled all war provisions. They themselves have performed nothing as productive men, neither have they taken part in the production, nor indeed participated actively in the war activities; they have only derived profit from every single thing, from blood and tears, from the horrors of the war, from the hunger of the masses, from the wastefulness of the nouveaux riches, from the speculative fury of the stock-exchange public. All that becomes gold and gold value to international finance. Every work of the productive nations brings interest to international finance. Even here, in the international economy, we have to do with a complete reversal of the correct and reasonable relationship between capital and work.

The workers work reasonably and offer their work products on the world market – in order to exchange them for foreign work products (raw products, semi- or fully fabricated). A reasonable economy is not appointed to exchange foreign currencies (dollar or English pound notes) for supplied optical instruments and to then cancel these and then speculate further in foreign currencies. In times of a healthy economy no factory owner would have thought of such a thing. He of course needs the proceeds for his further products, in order to be able to produce further, to pay his workers and to buy new raw materials. It is fully impossible that the entire German economy should collect its proceeds from its export of industrial products in the form of foreign currencies or in foreign exchange, for the same German total national economy must buy its raw material needs in cotton for the enormous textile industry, in copper for our likewise gigantic electrical industry, in silk, jute, tropical fruits, the increased demand, above the home production, in food and fodder, etc., to name just a few. The received amounts of foreign monies therefore have to be immediately disbursed again. This is also in itself quite natural, for in normal times one cannot do anything with foreign currencies in one's own country except exchange them. This is so even today. The American worker cannot be paid with French francs, and the English businessman is not paid in his shops with Italian liras. There is also no sense in taking the currencies to foreign countries where they cannot at all be used as legal means of payment. The local currency serves and should only serve the internal needs of the country that issues the currency. Just as, within a national economy, the meaning of goods production does not lie in trading in money and in then sitting on the money as it were and in withholding it from the economy, so too the international economic exchange of goods is completed only when import is paid for with export.

The theoretical ideal-situation would be now that every country could cover and pay for its import need exactly with its export. Then, and only then, can one speak of an absolute stability of foreign currencies. Now the effort of every upward striving national economy understandably is directed at achieving an export surplus over the import need. Only this indicates increase of wealth. Then one speaks of an active balance of trade. If the import need remains over the export, elements of the internal wealth must be delivered to foreign countries for the balancing of this deficit. But these deliveries must, since they cannot indeed be extracted from the work income, once again be taken only from the wealth. This occurs either through the export of gold or of securities. Especially the last "export" however is nothing but the beginning of the international interest slavery. Whether this "export of securities" extends to existing internal securities or is disguised in the form of foreign "bonds" is practically a matter of indifference for the nations affected by it. But since also, in the international economic thinking, only the profitability madness of large loan capital rules, all reasonable doubts of an honourable national economy are trampled down by means of the press and the parliaments, and the international slavery of all nations to the international finance making this bond spreads to a frightful scope.

III. The State

Even here in the international economy there are manifested the same phenomena as in the internal national economy and the frightful crises which shake the different national economies today are in the main a resulting phenomenon of this enslavement of all the nations of the western cultural circle, as we have already learnt above. The weak currency countries, whose internal economy has become too weak (Russia) or whose internal situation has become uncertain through revolution (Germany) and whose still gigantic production surpluses are confiscated free of cost as reparations from the enemy, have no more surplus purchasing power, they can therefore no longer pay for their import need with goods but with paper money which they throw in large quantities into foreign countries in order to buy foreign currency therewith. Thereby they harm in a similar way both the internal economy and also the foreign economies. The strong currency countries, on the other hand, choke precisely on the elevation of their currencies (Switzerland, for example). They can no longer export their products to the earlier large markets because their products are too expensive on account of the high exchange value of their money. These countries can cover their import need easily with their strong currency. But when the finished products are much cheaper in the countries with bad currency, the traders and profiteers go to the weak currency countries and buy out and rob these countries to the disadvantage of both countries – the disadvantage of the local production and the disadvantage of the consumption in the countries that are bought out, in which the already small inventory level of goods is reduced even further by these wild purchases. Thereby the purchasing power of the national currency in the weak currency countries once again sinks.

That, in view of these fully topsy-turvy relations, everything has not already long ago collapsed is due to the fact that, even above all the machinations of international finance, the mutual international need simply prevails. Only, everything happens at the last moment, with groaning and moaning, because the spanner – the interest demands of international capital - has been thrown into the works of the international economy. Or, expressed in medical imagery: In the healthy blood circulation of the international economy a, at first small, but today already enormously large, carcinoma has set in which has only a one-sided interest of sucking up all the blood into itself at the cost of the rest of the body and to take a transit toll, an interest, from everything. All the blood of course flows into the heart, but the heart gives out also with each beat the contaminated blood. The state bank which serves only the pure monetary transaction corresponds

The German State on a National and Socialist Foundation

precisely to this image – and to the carcinoma corresponds most precisely the activity of international finance, which also controls all the money of the world through its credit banks and holds the entire international economy gripped in its suction arms and takes interest everywhere. All this is not necessary! The nations of the world do not in any way need supranational financial powers. Obviously institutions are necessary which internationally regulate the international monetary transactions in the sense of a clearing house or in the sense of the postal cheque accounts. That can and will be taken care of by state-run foreign exchange offices.

In any case there are enough ways and means, quite similar to how it was possible to create an international postal union, to organise even the international payment transactions mainly through clearing, without the international finance benefiting two or three times in all these simple mercantile operations and becoming big and fat at the cost of the productive nations. Details are superfluous here.

The stabilisation of a currency cannot therefore, as emphasised, be separated from the inter-national relations. There is however a series of possibilities of removing the sources of error and the irresponsibilities that lie in the deficiencies of the internal administration or in the unrestricted manipulation of the note printing press.

The proposed measures all lie within the field of already tested systems; like the nationalisation of the Reichsbank and the central banks, they arise simply as the logical consequences of a new position of the state towards its tasks as the protector of the monetary transactions. They only represent the natural reaction to conditions that served merely and solely the interest of high finance at the greatest cost of the people. The sensible extension of the nationalisation of the Reichsbank is the regulation and mediation of the monetary transaction by the state according to the model of the postal cheque system, which will be further extended and more appropriately developed for this purpose.

All these measures indeed signify already quite powerful steps forwards, but they could be carried out also without the economic attitude having to be already basically transformed in the sense of the National Socialist principle presented with all emphasis: "The task of the economy is the covering of need and not the profitability of private capital".

III. The State

This fundamental transformation and new ordering in the field of the financial and tax system, as well especially in the financing of large state tasks with an avoidance of the loan route, as well as the financial political measures which indeed come close to the scope of functions of the field of social policy, will occupy us in the next chapter.

New Ways

The Financing of Large Public Works

Among the most important state tasks is the execution of quite large economic undertakings whose execution exceeds the capital resources of private entrepreneurial circles, in whose execution moreover considerable public-legal interests are concerned and whose execution is based on the exploitation of natural resources or natural energy sources. Tasks, therefore, in which the exploitation of natural forces which belong to the community is at issue, or whose execution has to occur within the range of the tasks that are mainly incumbent on the state, like the entire field of transport.

One sees that it is completely possible to limit the field rather precisely on which state initiative can be developed without limits being drawn thereby for the private entrepreneurial initiative or the state having to exert a competition to it. In addition there is, beyond this, the fact that the execution of these large public works is naturally assigned almost totally to private enterprises.

We have already described in detail in the fundamental observations in what an exemplary way the state has built up our German transport system. Certainly here and there it would have been more rationally and cheaply developed by private enterprise but, in the case of tasks in which the security of millions of men is at stake, it is not so much a question of that as of the greatest possible solidity. Now, the transport enterprise is definitely a purely state task. Reliability, punctuality, security, uniform tariffs for railways and post must be the decisive viewpoints for the transport system – and not – the profitability of private capital.

But this question is closely connected to the form of the financing of such large public tasks.

We have already seen the internal nonsense that is revealed in the fact that the "credits" approved by the parliament must be "approved" afterwards again by private capital, for which the state then has to take upon itself a quite extraordinary burden through the promise of interest. It will no longer be necessary here to point in a general way to the disastrous consequences of this promise of interest. The present work indeed serves mainly to prove this fact. Nevertheless, let a special reference be made here also to how extraordinarily more

III. The State

expensive, and in what an unbelievable way for everybody who hears these figures for the first time, this promise of interest on the state loans has made the railway tariffs, for instance.

The capital costs for the entire network of the German Reichsrailways, which were built or undertaken through loans, amounted to around 25 billion gold marks up to 1914. The interest payments for this amount, with an average interest of 3½ – 4%, amounted to around 800-900 million gold marks. The net revenues, after the deduction of the costs for personal (officials and employees) and material (coal and lubricants) expenses, amounted to around 800-1100 million marks.

The interest payment thus consumed almost the entire net revenue of the German railways. It was always a misleading of the public opinion when it was explained with a certain pride that the revenues from the post and railways formed the backbone of the state budget. Of course it could have been that, if only the interest payment had not consumed the entire net revenues. Another interesting parallel can be drawn in comparison, that is, that the total expenditures for wages and salaries to all the German railway officials and employees and to the railway workers in the plants, and on the line, taken together amounted to precisely only as much as this interest charge on loan capital did! In other words: the gigantic army of German railway workers up to the highest positions with a head count of 782,731 persons has received for its work only exactly as much income as the completely inactive hand of loan capital has pocketed.

This interest payment to loan capital just from the railways was greater than the entire expenditures for our entire large Reichsarmy of that time! - and indeed for everything that is connected with it, thus also including the military supervision, the military administration of justice, including the systems of garrison administration and military construction, the military education and development system, the technical institutes, the relief and military widows funds – and, further, the clothing and arming of the troops!!! The entire amount for our entire army amounted in 1913 – thus in the last full year of peace, to 775,385,300 marks. Such comparative figures provide a deep insight. While the socialist and democratic side constantly hustled against the "burden of the military armaments" in the parliamentary sessions and in the press, one also never finds even a single word against such interest burdens – far eclipsing all other expenses – from public loans. Indeed, one could have paid the entire navy too out of the interests for the loan for the general need. The entire expenses for our proud Reichsnavy amounted in 1913 to 197 million. And one should consider that all these expenses could have been defrayed without a penny if our state budget had not been burdened with such gigantic interest burdens. A handful of large loan capitalists – the couple of thousand 'hangers-on', of small savers with their possessions of a couple of thousand marks, do not at all play a role in such public loans – thus pocketed year in year out, fully without work or effort, amounts with which we could have maintained and paid our entire Reichsadministration, our entire army and our navy.

One who, in view of such figures, does not acquire an understanding of the all-surpassing importance of the interest problem in general and of the fully failed national financial policy with its loan economy in particular cannot indeed be helped. What is more, the figures and numbers which provide such an insight are accessible to everybody, they are found in the Statistical Yearbook for the German Reich published with the greatest conscientiousness by the former Royal Statistical Office and they are found likewise in the Statistical Yearbook for the German Reich, Puttkammer and Mühlbrecht Publishers, published by the Republican Statistical Reichsoffice.

That such imbalances between the necessary expenses for the Reichsadministration, the army and navy and the expenditures of the state for the interest payment to loan capital become an injustice crying to the heavens will however become fully clear only when we examine in what way then the Reich now covers its monetary need for these interest payments. Here we come to the field of customs and taxes. I must point here once again to the thorough representation of this situation in my book The coming tax strike, where I have produced the conclusive proof that the largest part of all the taxes is borne by the wide masses of the working population. We thus have the fact before us that the state at first, in complete disregard of the possibilities lying in its financial sovereignty, ventures on the loan route for the execution of large public tasks, that is, incurs debts; that it then thereby further burdens its budget in such a way that it must use all its net revenues for the interest payment and that it further must oppress the people with duties and taxes only in order to be able to meet its interest obligations. All essentially necessary state tasks it must now combat in the provincial- and Reichsparliament against the greatest resistance, and finally the state sees itself in the role of an interest-collector for the loan capital, as we see it today.

III. The State

The way out has already been pointed out a long time ago - after such a detailed examination of the present absurd conditions it is obvious; it is that:

> The state will finance all large public undertakings of the Reich by virtue of its financial sovereignty and after approval by the population through the parliament with the strictest avoidance of the loan route through direct allocation of means through cashless transfer transactions or through the issue of interest-free state treasury notes.

I can make this measure clear best through an example: the development of the Bavarian hydro-energy.

The plans and efforts to make the enormous hydro-energy existing in the mountain rivers, in combination with the large mountain lakes, useful date back to already more than two decades ago. Unquestionably, in the case of this hydro-energy, it was a matter of energy sources of the country which belong to the community and were to be taken from it and used for personal profit. Thus it is clear that, in the development of such large structures, many public and private legal interests were affected. It is a matter here of a field that belongs exclusively to the sphere of influence of the state. The people also now orally approved the credits through their representatives in December 1920. It had been sufficiently advised and tested and replanned repeatedly and one was fully clear about the great economic advantages. The state and the people had decided to exploit the energy sources, now they had, with this credit approval, simply to take the corresponding decision that the amounts earned by the entrepreneurs could be paid out directly by the state bank on the basis of the approved credits. Whether this would occur without cash, by way of transfer into the giro transactions, or through credit advice to postal cheque accounts or in cash is finally a matter of indifference.

It is really obvious and clear, if we imagine that the state bank for such purposes would issue its own money to the amount of the necessary and approved credits. These hydro-energy construction notes thus represented to a certain degree state treasury notes that would be issued to the rising water works as anticipatory credit under state guarantee. It was thus a matter of a money covered in manifold ways. The coverage consisted first in the ready or rising Walchensee work, etc. and secondly in the state guarantee that the money is accepted at full value from the public treasury instead of payment.

The German State on a National and Socialist Foundation

The construction notes would be at the same time partial debentures on the waterworks, without interest claims however being bound to them. This is however, as is well known, not the case with any other notes that are in circulation.

The hydro-energy construction notes could very well make these specifications on the full coverage of their value in the text of their imprint. For example: "This thousand mark note finds its coverage partially in the value of the installation being erected for the exploitation of the Bavarian hydro-energy. It is accepted in all state treasuries as payment".

If one wishes to go further, there stands nothing in the way of the state's pledging to provide, after the completion of the work, against the deposit of the note, so many kilowatt hours of electricity or so many hundredweights of nitrogen.

Nobody would refuse to accept such money issued by the state that is completely covered by material goods, that can at the same time be used to some extent as a ration coupon for electricity. On the contrary we may be sure that such a money would enjoy a special popularity, for this money is – stable, exactly as stable as a dollar, or much better because one can receive for it a quite definite amount of electricity or nitrogen – independent of economic fluctuations. It is a sign of the complete narrow-mindedness of men that in the public propaganda of different debaters the objection arose that - "nobody would accept this money". No man has ever hesitated, even these debating gentlemen – to accept money that the state has issued. Everybody has accepted even the most damaged paper money of the Reichsbank even though this money was pure inflation money. And yet everybody accepted it, even when the clever speculators tried to get rid of it as quickly as possible against foreign currency or goods. Indeed, nobody has refused even the emergency currency of cities and communities that was similarly uncovered paper money. And now should such a preferable covered paper money as the construction money completely covered by material assets is for our large works not be accepted immediately? Surely, even those who raise such objections against interest-free government money on behalf of, or in the spirit of, their masters do not basically believe that. It is indeed proven to be irrefutable, in spite of all the complaints of the "metallists" who would like to consider as money only money made of precious metals, that "money" is that which the state declares to be money – whether this money is constituted of paper or porcelain, iron or leather or

III. The State

any other material is a matter of complete indifference. It is quite different when it comes to the purchasing power of this money. There the metallists are right that a currency made of gold by and large retains its exchange value even when political disturbances shake the state. This stability, however, the metallic money made of precious metals does not owe to its monetary character but to its character as a commodity, namely gold.

There can be no doubt at all about the justification of the state in covering its monetary need for a large work in the way described. First, the state is sovereign, that is, it does not need to be influenced by anybody, for it has the power, and, secondly, such a measure can stand up to the strictest commercial examination. The state issues with this cash in a way vouchers on the basis of its credit. Why should anybody have less regard for the credit of the state than for the credit of any banks, especially when the state is producing useful works for the welfare of the community. Even if one said that the state however pays the performed work (the entrepreneurs and workers who are engaged in the Walchensee work) with paper, that is indeed right because later, after the completion of the works, the state accepts this paper once again as payment for the work performed by it (supply of electricity or nitrogen, etc.). Therewith the economic cycle is completed. The construction notes are thus once again redeemed from the electricity supplies, etc. of the first years, the notes are destroyed, and a gigantic work of governmental organisational art has been created in an interest-free way as an interest-free possession for all. A work that has tapped, without a great burdening of the electricity consumers, another large source of money for the state which brings the state in turn closer to the ideal goal of a healthy national financial policy – the state without taxes.

Now, there is, in addition, the fact that the described process with the issue of one's own construction money for a certain work does not at all necessitate the issue of the entire approved amount in such construction notes, because indeed by far the largest part of the payments to the entrepreneurs does not occur in cash but cash-free, through transfers. But, even assuming the case that one issued the entire new construction amount in new state bank notes, these amounts in comparison with the other amounts that the state today needs would not at all be considerable. At the same time that one broke one's head in the Bavarian parliament on account of the 800 million credit for the Bavarian hydro-energy – or better: did not break but just resorted once again to "loan" -, 8,000 million was approved in the parliament "without debate in the third reading for the purposes of the general emergency".

Here I recall once again the considerations that, in the case of such a financing through the new issue of money, no inflation of any sort would be brought about, that on the other hand the issue of interest-bearing bonds during the construction period in any case signifies a certain inflation since interests must already be paid even though though no productive work is yet performed by the works.

In no way however is the national economic balance between money and material goods, in the sense of the quantity theory, affected for, against the increase of means of payment on the side of money, there stands an exactly greater increase in goods. If then later, through the revenues of such works, the issued money is once again withdrawn and destroyed, then the national economic balance is naturally improved to the advantage of the national wealth according to the total value of such new works.

Even here let it be pointed out how severely the interest operates on the costs of the products of such works. Oskar Pöbing[90] has determined in a detailed examination of this question that the production costs for a kilowatt hour are made more expensive through the burdening of the loans with interest to the enormous amount of 500% (!). Now the electricity from our Bavarian Hydro-electric works comes to us five times more expensively because we have once again resorted to the loan route that lies "closest at hand". Even here it is appropriate to imagine that the entire material and personal expenses for the operation and maintenance of the large Bavarian electric works and interurban offices - thus all the wages and salaries for all persons occupied in these works - sluice attendants, machinists, workers, labourers, supervisory personnel, and further the entire technical and commercial administrative apparatus up to the directors together draw for their work year in year out only a fifth part of the amounts that the - so very good - loan capitalists draw year in year out, without effort or work - as interest.

Interest devours everything, interest makes everything more expensive. Only loan capital has the benefit, the population has

---

90 [Oskar Pöbing (1882-1956) was a Bavarian mechanical engineer who worked in the Technical University in Munich. He was the author of studies such as *Die Wasserkräfte Bayerns* (1919) and *Zur Bestimmung strömender Flüssigkeitsmengen in offenen Gerinnen* (1922).]

III. The State

the damage. The population that builds the works through its own strength has the damage; for who then builds the Bavarian works? - indeed Bavarian engineers, Bavarian workers, Bavarian foremen and entrepreneurs; Bavarian factories supply most of the machines and equipment – and for that which is not produced in Bavaria itself Bavarian grain or cattle must be given, thus Bavarian work must once again be given in exchange – only the Bavarian people do not put up the money for the construction (apparently!), and so for that it needs the large capitalists from New York and London, Paris and Berlin. The Bavarian people must borrow from all the countries of the world and burden its hydro-energy with an interest payment which makes the electricity 500% more expensive!

Is this not madness? Is this not an economic crime? of the people who have done nothing but at one time set their pen in motion and written out a cheque or directed their banker to sign the Bavarian hydro-electric loan, these receive for that, year after year, interests paid by the Bavarian people.

Not only that but the waterworks are therewith no longer a free possession of the Bavarian people but they are pledged to the capitalist. Especially funny is, further, the situation that the large capitalists would naturally not lend "their good money" to a state which is not in itself "good" for capital and interests, which therefore still enjoys so much credit that one can pump 800 million into it. And in fact the tenders for the hydro-electric bonds contained the guarantee that is so enticing and assuring to the capitalists "that the Bavarian state with its entire wealth guarantees for capital and interests - (!)"

Moneybag, what more do you want! So here the Bavarian state admits quite expressly that it is worth so much, that one could loan to it 800 million for the Walchensee hydro-energy and the Middle Isar but – it cannot use its financial sovereignty and finance these works through its own authority. Why?? Because it is too deeply enmeshed in the loan and interest madness, because its responsible statesmen do not have so much thinking capacity and feeling of responsibility of their own that they dare to judge these simple and clear plans for an interest-free financing by themselves; they therefore turn to the professional banking experts. This is exactly as if a consumptive were to ask his tuberculosis bacilli whether they thought it right that he go to Davos or to Engadin[91] in order to get rid of his illness, and these assured

---

91 [Davos in Switzerland has, since the middle of the 18th century, been famed

The German State on a National and Socialist Foundation

him: "No, just do not do this, the journey could harm you, perhaps a railway accident may occur, rather stay at home in your house, in your usual environment. In your condition you should not make any experiments! etc". With the adherence to this advice that is from the viewpoint of the tuberculosis bacilli quite right, the consumption naturally makes a ripping progress, the bacilli multiply wonderfully. Exactly so in our case of the financial and interest economy.

This getting advice from one's own opponents is extremely characteristic of the unsuspecting Germans. If a man appears who loves his people passionately and advices them this and that and alerts the responsible men to this or that knavery, one can bet ten to one that the concerned people would run to the knave and ask him quite naively: "Tell me, so and so has told me that you are a rascal, please tell me if that is right!" And if the other then explains to him with the most honest face in the world: "But what do you think then – I a scoundrel! - on the contrary, I am your best friend, I have always helped you out of our financial difficulties", then the guileless questioner is quite happy – he has done enough and he is especially glad that he does not have to strain his brain. The troublesome friend of the people, however, he does not in general deem worthy of his answer – and things are further stuck in the rut of the interest capitalistic loan policy until the last item of free national wealth is pledged to the financial powers and the entire nation only pays interest to the international finance.

In conclusion we must, precisely in this context, further point to the fact that the Bavarian state – when it was not in any way a matter of such an important state task as the development of the Bavarian hydro-energy however is, that is, when it was a matter of remedying the monetary crisis of the November government - was very prompt in issuing from the Bavarian state bank around 130 million state treasury notes of the Bavarian State Bank. This happened completely uncovered – and everybody took these Bavarian notes exactly as willingly as the notes of the Reichsbank, and everybody could buy for himself as much bread for the Bavarian vouchers as for the Reichsbank notes. Indeed, it did not even have to be the entire Bavarian state, it was enough if the mayor of the provincial capital Munich and some city elders had their names printed on such colourful bits of paper, and even this emergency money circulated, everybody took it and everybody gave it out exactly like the scraps of the Reichsbank, and

---

as a medical resort for those suffering from lung diseases. Engadin is a valley in the Swiss Alps.]

III. The State

this emergency money itself fulfilled the task of any money – of being an aid for the exchange of goods - in an unobjectionable way.

Only one office was extremely unpleasantly affected by these artificial pieces of the provinces and communities – high finance – and they forced a Reich law in October 1921 according to which it was strictly forbidden to the provinces and communities to issue emergency money any further. This law was in its effect a clear law for the protection of the Jews, which was to be followed in 1922 by the "Law for the protection of the republic".

I can very well imagine the sudden fear of international finance when they recognised that in the interest-free money, even in the harmless form of emergency money, the people held in their hand a weapon – naturally without the people knowing this – which could with one stroke tear apart the golden network established with lies and deception through centuries-long underground and counterfeit work and liberate the peoples from their interest slavery.

Already at that time, in the case of the issue of the Bavarian state money, the Reichsbank demanded very soon that this money had to be withdrawn once again, which also then occurred in a compliant manner in the course of 1921. The reason: this money brought high finance no interests as the money of the Reichsbank does through the indirect route of the Reich's treasury bills.

In the National Socialist state, in future all large state tasks will be financed and organised in the way described with a total avoidance of the loan route. We shall naturally take the indirect route of the interest-free construction money in general only if the necessary means cannot be raised from the surpluses of other state enterprises or from special levies for such special purposes. In any case we know that this form of financing opens quite undreamt of and enormous possibilities of tapping the natural resources of the country, improving the transport routes, etc.

Every nation is as rich as it is able to organise work.[92]

---

[92] This is reflected in Hitler's speech to the Reichstag on January 30, 1939 in which he declared: "Under the compulsion of ... need we have learned in the first place to take full account of the most essential capital of a nation, namely, its capacity to work." (quoted in R de Roussy de Sales (ed.) *Adolf Hitler: My New Order,* London: Angus and Robertson, 1942, p.457f.).

The Social Construction - And Economic Bank

In logical connection with the previous chapter stands the creation of a social construction- and economic bank which has the task of issuing interest-free construction money especially for the construction of houses. Of course this social construction - and economic bank should not be conducted as a state institution but as a corporation of public law. Logically therefore the discussion of it should come after the representation of the National Socialist tax system, but since this social construction- and economic bank is nothing but the interest-free financing transferred to the conditions of the private economy and indeed especially to the housing construction system – thus a branch of the economy of the most universal significance –, placing it first is perhaps justified.

Why such a construction bank should not be conducted as a pure state enterprise is due to the fact that such a public legal financial institution must be more freely manoeuvrable than a state enterprise can be. It would not be so much of a reason if it was a matter of only mere housing construction, but there will be many cases where it is a matter of tasks of the greatest importance which indirectly affect the public interest, and then the bank, which is indeed responsible in its leadership to the state for its management, should and must have a free hand in issuing also interest-free credit after a thorough examination of all conditions.

Such a freedom of decision however is not possible in purely state enterprises. That is why this must be left to private initiative. By way of illustration may be presented here the sketch of such a law which was passed in 1922 for Bavaria:

Law on the development of a Bavarian social construction- and economic bank.

Art.1 A national Bavarian social construction - and economic bank (BWB) shall be founded.

The BWB has the task of financially supporting enterprises of the state or national economically valuable enterprises of private persons (whether it be individuals or societies) which serve the development of the country or are beneficial to the general welfare.

Art.2 The BWB is a corporation of public law. The more detailed

III. The State

prescriptions regarding its organisation, its administration and activity and its directorship will be decreed by the entire ministry.

Art.3 Permission is granted to the BWB to issue at first interest-free treasury notes covered by material assets to an amount of up to 50 million gold marks.

The issue may occur only in such a legal way that the amount of the money amounts issued at any time and in circulation is covered by material securities of at least the same value (interest-free security mortgages, security bills of sale, hypothecations, etc.) and the repayment or the return of the treasury notes is secured by the revenues of the enterprises or institutions to be developed within an appropriate time-limit, at most 50 years.

Art.4 The sum of the pledges and securities due to the issued treasury notes of the BWB constitutes the coverage association of the BWB.

Legal transactions of any sort which disturb or harm a security or property coverage belonging to the coverage association are void.

Property - or possession changes of any sort to objects or rights subject to the coverage organisation do not affect the existence of the securities and remain attached to the object even for the new purchaser; the predecessor in title is freed of personal liability only when the BWB agrees to the change in the person of the debtor. Contrary arrangements are void..

Art.5 The entire constituents and rights of the coverage organisation of the BWB is recorded in this public register; the principles and legal consequences are valid for this book correspondingly as for registers; the register has public confidence and the presumption of right in itself.

Access to the register or the pertinent sections of it is to be granted to everybody who evidences a legal interest in the access.

Balance-like summaries are to be published annually on the total amounts of the issued treasury notes, as well as the total amount of the securities due to the BWB for these, as well as additions and deductions, and on the successful repayments and redemptions of treasury notes.

Art.6 The treasury notes of the BWB are legal currency. Everybody has to accept them at the full rate of their face value against the exchange rate of the other legal currencies of the state. If a creditor refuses the acceptance of treasury notes of the BWB instead of payment at the above mentioned minimum rate of exchange, the debtor is, insofar as he has actually offered the payment in treasury notes, freed of the debt of this amount.

The BWB issues the treasury notes interest-free and agrees upon, in a contract, the general and special conditions of the mutual legal conditions regarding the periods and rates of the issue, the securities and mortgages to be paid by the debtor, as well as the repayments and other pertinent legal conditions. A copy of these contracts is to be made accessible to all as an appendix to the entries in the register of the coverage association.

The BWB is justified in determining surcharges or fees for the administrative costs in the commitment of loans and for the yearly collections or in determining corresponding premiums or discounts at any time in a uniform public manner.

The issue or the stock-exchange quotation of a higher rate than the minimum rate determined in Art.1 is permissible.

The repayments can be made only in treasury notes of the same sort as those issued.

Art.7 The activity of the BWB, insofar as it extends to the observation of the prescriptions contained in this law, is subject to the control and supervision of a public supervisory council consisting of the Finance Minister or a representative to be named by him, the Minister of the Interior or a representative to be named by him, the Justice Minister or a representative to be named by him and three persons to be elected from the parliament for a duration of two years.

Art.8 Penalty clause: Imprisonment penalties for intentional damages to the securities of the coverage association and likewise for commercial or customary, especially stock-exchange, sabotage of the construction bank notes or the exchange rate value of the same or for an attempt to do so. In addition, high monetary penalties for this, even to juristic persons.

In the "executive conditions" precise prescriptions were then issued

III. The State

on the constitution of the board of directors and the advisory board to which belong representatives of the ministries, the parliament and the builders. The task of such an advisory board is the control of the legal use of the construction notes, the examination of the repayments, further the verification of the hypothecary indemnities, the approval of the bases of the mortgaging with interest-free construction notes, etc.

The further conditions then regulated the repayment and clearance, the stock-postings on the issued series of construction notes and on the securities registered for it, and, further, more prescriptions on the approved construction designs, etc. At that time the inducement to the establishment of such a social bank was provided by the enormous housing need and the circumstance that the Reich and provinces could not in any way control the distress in an effective way. The concerned institutions of housing offices could of course free up living spaces here and there – but they could not build any new housing. The new construction activity suffered from a lack of materials, above all from the fact that, with the existing emergency control of rents, the construction of new houses was absolutely "unprofitable" for private capital.

The grants given by the Reich and the provinces for the coverage of the so-called lost construction-expenditure were not sufficient by far in the progressing currency devaluation. Even the individual housing constructions begun here and there could not remove the general housing distress. Even the creation of cheap mortgage monies was impossible because, with the rents fixed at that time, even the cheapest construction money precluded a 4% interest.

It happens therefore that, as already suggested in the fundamental observations, in spite of the greatest need – on account of insufficient profitability – the need is simply not covered.

Now then, if one succeeds in removing the annually recurring interest burdens, if one makes provisions to place interest-free means at the disposal of those needing housing, a stimulation of the housing market in a grand style is possible. Therewith however would not only the frightful housing need with all its social and health damages be removed but also the internal market would be stimulated in an extraordinary manner because all the innumerable ancillary trades, the locksmiths, carpenters, roofers, plumbers, the glaziers, installers, ceramists, the floor-layers and tilers, the painters and plasterers

The German State on a National and Socialist Foundation

depend on it, they then for their part find work and bread and are strengthened in their purchasing capacity.

This means however is offered in the interest-free construction money.

These construction notes are issued by the "Social Construction- and Economic Bank". The suppliers and entrepreneurs are paid for the construction with this money. The building owner pays the received interest-free money back in appropriate instalments within a period of 30-50 years according to the character and durability of the construction. The construction notes are different from the Reichs- or provincial money rather in same manner that the Reichsbank notes were different from the loan treasury notes. These construction notes find, as already mentioned, their full material coverage in the fact that, at the same time there arise, to the credit of the construction bank, equal in amount to the issued notes, new material assets (houses) which are legally secured through the registration of interest-free mortgages to the same amount.

Practically also here the full value of the new buildings will not be given in construction notes but only the actual building expenditure. The land will therefore have to be made available at least by the builders or the building societies or the communities and, beyond this, at least 10-30% of the building value must be produced by those in need of housing, of which 5% is to be retained there for the coverage of the administrative costs of the construction bank.

The repayment then follows without further calculation of any interest. In this manner the free property of the house-owners grows from year to year in their houses and likewise the values retained within the total association as coverage for the issued construction notes. Thereby the amount of construction notes in circulation diminishes according to the repayments effected.

The legal character of this construction money is nothing other than the issue of a bond. The debtor of this bond is the construction bank. The creditor of a bond is the current owner of this bond.

Nobody can be forbidden to issue bonds, it is always only a question of the external circumstances, whether the bonds issued by somebody are accepted generally as payment. As mentioned many times before, the construction notes are always and under any conceivable economic and political condition fully covered by the material assets against

III. The State

these. There can therefore be no question of the bank's falling into difficulties at any time.

The universal acceptance is however guaranteed the moment that the state pledges to assume the guarantee for the time-limited redemption of the construction notes and, during the duration the notes, to accept the notes in their registers as payment or when they are declared to be legal means of payment.

Such an acceptance of the guarantee now does not mean for the state, practically, the least burdening; on the contrary. Today the state must actually spend and pay interest on, and then recoup through general taxes, uncounted millions yearly for the grants approved by it for lost construction expenditure. This is then fully cancelled.

The grants now given by the state are thus really lost money which must be recouped by the community, and which go to some lucky people who were indeed able to grab such grants.

Thus even when a delinquent payer among the receivers of interest-free construction notes actually at some time cannot meet his obligations, this does not play any role in relation to the enormous savings which the state budget makes because it also does not, in this way, have to make any sacrifices that are fully lost.

Since it is a question of a task of great social significance, it is justified to establish an independent public legal corporation as the instrument and bearer of its execution.

In this way this institution will be removed from the sphere of the private economic social forms to which naturally personal profits and enrichment intentions are attached in the eyes of the people. On the other hand, the institution will be removed from the domain of the pure state enterprise, against which likewise, not entirely without injustice, a certain aversion exists in all economic matters among the public.

In the implementational regulations everything is to be recorded that is basically indispensable for the public and for the security of the business management of the bank.

The proposed advisory council can make its influence felt beyond this. The advisory council itself is again a reflection of all the interest groups concerned.

The establishment of a construction bank as a public legal corporation also has the pleasant by-effect that in this way the entire complex of the wealth values created in this manner does not appear as the property of the state but as the property of an independent legal entity, which is the construction bank.

The juridical construction or the legal character of this construction bank is thus the following: The construction bank is a legal entity by virtue of the circumstance that it is recognised or established as a public legal corporation; this construction bank does not at all consist of individual members; it is in itself the bearer of the rights and duties that are developed from its activity. It is however also not an official and not a state institution, not a member of a state organism.

The creation of such a legal form is indeed not something common and traditional; but nevertheless something already provided for in the law; the present-day conditions however demand corresponding institutions of a modern sort. Herein indeed will lie the service when something of this sort is established: that, in a certain way, one goes beyond the limits of the traditional in order to adapt to the demands of the age.

How the conduct of the businesses proceeds is to be explained best with an individual example: The construction bank makes known in advance the fundamentals and preconditions which must be fulfilled if a request for approval of construction-bank money is to be considered. The applicant directs his request with the necessary documents to the construction-bank and, in affirmative cases, concludes a contract with those in need of housing (house owners).

In this contract is to be provided in the first place everything that the construction-bank ordinance and implementation regulations prescribe, thus the obligation to use the construction money only for the construction of the building, the obligation to a mortgage status and the repayment obligations. But, furthermore, all other pursuant legal conditions are to be laid down in this contract. It must especially be determined that the one in need of housing is not justified in selling the property again, which is moreover already highlighted practically in the mortgage order. The conditions for the devolution of inheritance and for the case of default of payment are to be regulated correspondingly with one or more repayment instalments.

(Details arise from the nature of this matter).

III. The State

Because all delivery firms and all workers are paid only in construction-bank notes which the construction bank itself produces, construction bank notes come into circulation for the first time in all circumstances only to the extent that the equivalent in payments accrues to the property. From the workers and suppliers the construction-bank notes reach the public; in consideration of the existing securities and especially because the state assumes the guarantee for the construction-bank notes and state treasuries accept the construction-bank notes as payment, the public will accept the construction-bank notes like any other money. So it remains left to the house owner how he fulfils his obligation to the construction-bank of repaying annually 2% of the loaned amounts in construction-bank notes. In other words, the building owner and mortgage debtor of the construction-bank must produce every year 2% in construction-bank notes from the amounts found in circulation. Practically it will happen that the mortgage debtors will collect construction-bank notes which indeed circulate along with the local money before the expiry date of their repayment dues and therewith satisfy their payment obligation. A specially suited place where to get construction-bank notes will be the construction sites that are to be found in operation at any time.

If one supposes, in order to have an idea, that in a year construction-bank notes are issued in Munich for 10 million, from this annually 200,000 gold marks will return to the construction-bank; thus, after 50 years at most, the entire 10 million will have returned and been collected by the construction bank, after 50 years at most the houses built from it are therewith repaid and become the debt-free property of their owners. The entire payment has occurred without a penny being paid uselessly for interests; the payment is further accomplished through nothing but the simple means of the establishment of the construction-bank, bound with the state guarantee.

The social act consists in the fact that the state has produced the value of the houses absolutely from nothing, that it created an income for thousands of workers and businessmen through the construction of this entire building. If one supposes that it is a matter of thousands of individual houses, thousands of landless are therewith transformed into landed persons.

Different objections and reservations will be made, of which the most important may be suggested:

a) The objection of inflation. This objection is as short-sighted as it is irrelevant; as already explained in earlier passages, an inflation can arise only where uncovered money is issued. Here the material coverage stands against the construction-bank notes; it is therefore inconsequential if even considerable amounts of construction-bank notes come into circulation.

b) The objection that this matter is new and untested. This objection is actually inapplicable, and the matter is new perhaps for Germany. Elsewhere, one is used to such interest-free debt certificates covered by material assets. The typical example of this is the English warrant which was introduced a hundred years ago and is still preserved. The warrant is an order that gives the owner the right to a certain amount of crude iron lodged in a certain central storehouse. These warrant notes are used as currency; the purchasing power of the warrant has only those fluctuations to which the crude iron price is subjected on the world market.

If we had in Germany, for example, such warrants, these would have been completely independent of the German currencies and their fluctuations. The value of these warrants was related to the crude iron price, and the value of these prices in turn was automatically regulated in relation to the currency.

In the warrant we find the significant example of the popular nature of this interest-free debt certificate and debt-order covered by a material asset.

Insofar as considerable and national economically important erections of new buildings must be realised, it is imperative to construct entire colonies in series.

It would be a defective viewpoint if one wished to construct individual houses or even terrace houses only when the person looking for a house himself wishes to become an owner. The damage that has to be remedied is the housing distress, it is thus not a matter mainly of housing but it is a matter primarily of the creation of housing opportunities. This need will also be remedied by the fact that the commercial construction of rental flats is promoted. Nothing therefore prevents a rental house owner of the old style from receiving construction-bank notes for the construction of a new rental house. Precisely in the case of such persons it will be possible to demand in advance in cash a greater prepayment than only 10% of the entire building value; many of these people are ready and in a position to spend considerable sums of money from their own means for housing construction if they receive as a grant a corresponding remainder or partial amount interest-free from the construction-bank. Precisely the interest-free nature of the construction-bank money makes it possible to take into consideration this aspect of the revival of the building market that is so extremely important for big cities.

This social construction- and economic bank however will also pass over later beyond the limits of the financing of housing buildings to issuing interest-free credits to national economically important undertakings, industries, communal works, improvements in agriculture, etc., even if with a shorter repayment time-limit.

The State Without Taxes

The main goal of the National Socialist state is: the state without taxes. If this may sound under the present-day circumstances like a mad utopia, if it may seem to many as a promise that is too good to be true, we know nevertheless that this goal is completely reachable, at least insofar as the enormous tax pressure must be removed from the population.

With all clarity have we presented in the preceding chapters the proof that today almost all taxes are devoured just by interest payment. We pay taxes in every piece of bread that we eat, every warm parlour costs an excess of taxes, ever purchase is burdened with the sales tax. But everything that goes into taxes in this way is not, by far, sufficient to pay the taxes on the reparation debts alone.

It always betrays a lack of taste and critical understanding if one dismisses such a principal goal as doubtlessly the state without taxes is as a utopia. For one who has gone with us on the wide and convoluted paths of the present-day financial politics and one who has not lost the Ariadne thread – the interest obligation of the state – it must be an easy thing to find also the way out of this labyrinth of the Minotaur.

One who raises himself above the degradations and surveys from an elevated standpoint the connections described: interest obligation of the state – tax – inflation, one who has recognised the interest obligation of all nations of the western cultural circle as the fact dominating everything, one who has recognised that we live in an age of a complete reversal of the healthy and reasonable conditions

The German State on a National and Socialist Foundation

between work and wealth, one who can no longer avoid the pressing logic that especially the state, by virtue of its financial sovereignty, is not completely bound to the loan route but that it can creatively finance through its own right all large public state tasks, for him it is only the last step into a financial political New World to demand a state in which the state financial administration does not consider it as its first task to extract as much tax as possible from the state citizens but, on the contrary, to remove every burdensome tax pressure and to fertilise the national economy.

We are in a position to present the numerical evidence that the state without taxes is not at all a utopia but that the possibility of that is given in every orderly state budget if the state frees itself from the interest burden lying upon it. That it can do this also without it being called to account for it is proved by the history of state bankruptcies which relates dozens of cases in which the states have through bankruptcy escaped from the interest and debt burdens lying upon them.

It would take us too far afield to go into detail here once again into the precise demonstration that I have given in my small polemical work, The state bankruptcy: The solution, that, namely, the adjustment of the interest payment from the public loans in a simultaneous transformation of the bonds into interest-free bank assets does not in any way deserve the disreputable name of bankruptcy but that this form of liberation of the state and people from its interest-bound debt actually signifies the freedom of the state and economy from unbearable chains.

An adjustment of these interest payments however would have made possible, already before the war, the coverage of state expenses for the entire state administration. I have presented the Bavarian state budget of 1911 as an example. At that time, the revenues of the Bavarian state from the so-called commercial state enterprises (railways, post and telegraph) amounted to 120 million gold marks, the revenues from the state forestry 40 million. The total expenses for the entire state administration for the administration of justice (all district courts with their entire personnel and material expenses, all provincial courts, the regional courts and the highest law courts in Munich, Nuremberg, etc.) amounted to 27 million. For the entire large and so carefully developed internal administration of the entire Bavarian state - thus for the numerous district courts, for the county governments, for the police department of Munich, for the gendarmerie, further for the numerous other bodies and authorities like the medical authorities,

III. The State

the provincial vaccination hospital, the research institutions for food and semi-luxury foods, the sanatoriums and mental asylums, the administrative court, the provincial statistical office, the metrological authorities, the insurance chambers, etc. -, in 1911, 40 million was disbursed in the state budget. For education, school and church, thus especially for all the middle schools, the secondary schools, the preparatory schools, the Latin schools, the secondary education schools, the junior high schools, the higher vocational schools, the teacher training institutions, for all the state construction schools and specialist schools, the trade and music schools, the agricultural and district farming schools, for Weihenstephan[93] and for the biological research institute, for all the women's educational institutes, and then, above all, for the universities with their innumerable collections and institutes, the technical university, for the other arts universities, for the trade universities, for the academy of music, then for the Maximilianeum,[94] further for the central institutes for science and art, the academy of sciences, the scientific collections of the state, the Bavarian museums, the state library, the state theatre, etc., for these enormous field of activities of the Ministry of Culture with its thousands of officials, with its enormous art treasures in the collections and museums, all of which indeed require buildings, administration and care, in 1911, 51 million in all were disbursed. Within the field of the Finance Ministry, which indeed does not merely exercise functions that extract money from the people, lie the activities of the forest administration with hundreds of foresters, further the administration of mines, smelting works, salt works, the entire central and subsidiary customs offices, the central minting office, the state debt administration and the state bank, further the surveyor's offices and the provincial surveying office, then also the state spa administrations, the court brewery office, Munich, etc. This likewise very large enterprise caused an expense of 15 million. The expenses of the Transport Ministry were covered by its own operational revenues, on the other hand, the pensions of the old civil servants demanded further the very high amount of around 36 million.

Thus altogether the justice administration, the internal administration including the buildings - which I have not specifically mentioned

---

93 [Weihenstephan is an 11th century cloister in Upper Bavaria that was transformed in 1803 into a forestry school and state brewery.]

94 [The Maximilianeum in Munich was designed by King Maximilian II of Bavaria as the seat of a students' foundation. Since 1949 it has housed the Bavarian state parliament.]

above – and also the finance administration, as well as the education and development, and the pensions demanded 27+40+51+13+36=167 million.

The surpluses that the state enterprises, post and railways, mines and forests, delivered to the state treasury at around 160 million would thus have actually almost sufficed to cover the entire gigantic state administrative apparatus – without a penny of taxes!

The state without taxes would thus have been a reality, if the total taxes extracted from the Bavarian people, that is, 60 million of direct taxes and 53 million of indirect taxes, and in addition 31 million fees, altogether thus 134 million, had not had to be used completely for the interest payment to loan capital. The interest payment for the Bavarian state debts alone demanded 84.6 million (!) and Bavaria had to deliver 50 million to the Reich likewise for the interest payment from the Reich's debt.

I have given a brief overview of the large and small fields of our state life. This appears also especially important because National Socialism also bears in mind how extraordinarily much and how much exemplary work the old state performed, much that requires no reform and no improvement insofar as it does not have to do with matters that can never be concluded. Even for every state organism it is true that it cannot stand still if it does not wish to become ossified. In many a field a fresher and freer spirit will not harm, and here and there thorough reforms are appropriate. In many branches of our administrative apparatus at least a new spirit must enter, especially the spirit of the definite responsibility of the civil servant with regard to his tasks and the people whom he serves.

Only one field was forced into completely false ways – the state financial administration. If such circumstances as the ones just described are possible, this is indeed a sign that here a radical change must be effected. Now this is true, however, already for the state before the war – already at that time the state was yoked into the interest service for the private loan capital. Nothing reveals in a more striking manner the dependency of the state on loan capital already existing at that time than a survey of the distribution of the taxes on the different forms of income. According to the budget for 1911, that we have based our observations up to now upon, landed property was assessed at 12.6 million, house property at 12.1 million, the commercial enterprises at 17 million, but on the other hand, capital pensions with a total pension

III. The State

income of 253 (!) million gold marks at only 10 million. This is thus really an extremely indulgent treatment of those who can live without effort and work at the cost of the working population.

The myriad small pension incomes – we are thinking thereby of the pension group of 70-700 million marks – represent indeed in numbers the predominant mass of capital pension tax obligations, that is, around 150,000, but neither their income from capital interests nor their tax payment, at around 0.7 million, would play a role in the state budget – but what makes these figures so noteworthy for us is the circumstance that the large loan capital has created in these hundred thousands of small interest receivers a powerful protective guard against all attacks against the effort- and work-free income from interest.

It is naturally easy to persuade these small interest receivers that their savings must guarantee to a certain extent a lasting claim to interests, for the similarity of these people who have toiled their whole life long and have actually worked for their savings to the pension receivers in the state- and employees' conditions is obvious. But what differentiates this attitude from the idea of a pension is the essential difference that the pension claim depends on the person and is terminated at death, whereas the interest claim is a material one and is bound independently of the person in an impersonal way to the bare possession of money as an "eternal legal claim".

We shall deal with these connections further in the discussion of the general old age pensions, because these observations would allow us to find the transition from unjustified eternal interest to the justified claim of every national comrade to a care-free old age.

These small interest receivers do not come into consideration in the question that we are dealing with of the remarkable indulgent treatment of loan capital on the part of the old state, but only those who swallow the lion's share of the capital pensions and who then step forth again as the great financial donors of the state.

So away with this national economic nonsense of a interest-capitalistically oriented state financial administration and out into the free National Socialist state of work and performance freed of all taxes.

Once the state is freed of the lead-weight of its interest obligations, then one will see what the state can achieve. If new sources of revenue of a large scope come in addition, like the tapping of hydro-energy and the natural resources of the country, then the state without taxes will really no longer be a utopia but a joyful reality.

If we nevertheless wish to speak of a tax policy of the National Socialist state, this is because from such tax sources the means could flow for many tasks which actually await a state solution, for which however there were never any more means in the state budget. We are thinking here of the broad fields of national health, the fight against venereal diseases, alcohol abuse, the promotion of physical sports, the more substantial promotion of art and science, maternity leave, children's care, the construction of garden-cities and above all the acquittance of the debt of honour of the German people to its war-wounded and war-widows and orphans.

The following should be taken as guiding principles for a National Socialist state system in the field of tax policy:

1. A taxation for purposes of interest payment for internal loans is excluded.

2. Taxes are only permissible for the coverage of state expenditures for unproductive purposes, for administration, administration of justice, the military, police and health system and education, insofar as the surpluses of the commercial state enterprises, the railways, post, telegraph, state forests and state mines, as well as the electricity supply from the large state inter-urban bases, do not suffice for their coverage.

3. For the coverage of special needs or for special emergencies, thus especially for the case of war, direct and indirect taxes are not only permissible but commanded.

4. Direct taxes can be placed on property in any form, but here a far-reaching gradation is to be planned. The income is to be left tax-free up to an appropriate extent. In this case it should be considered more thoroughly than up to now whether the tax-payer has a family with children or other care duties.

5. State officials are basically to be left freed of taxes. For married people children's allowances are to be guaranteed.

6. Indirect taxes come into consideration in normal times only for

III. The State

luxury objects. The state has herein an excellent means at hand of operating in a way that would control and increase the prices on the production of articles that serve only the nuisance of attractive luxury, lavishness and gluttony in eating and drinking, and the excesses of fashion. Even pure semi-luxury goods like tobacco, alcohol, wine, insofar as they do not serve health purposes, will bear indirect taxes. On the other hand, all indirect taxes, such as exploit the people today in its entirety, are to be fundamentally avoided. We mean here all the nonsensical indirect taxes that operate only in a price-increasing manner, on sugar, salt, matches, lamps, lemonade, also the taxes on coal that make the production radically more expensive, also the taxes on personal and goods transport, and above all the commodity sales taxes.

7. The collection of war- and revolution profits are to be carried out as a task of justice. For such a task naturally the foundation of a reasonable basis of calculation on which one can compare the present wealth with the earlier must first be created. Obviously, here too a difference is to be made again between the wealth that arises from productive work, for which the war however signified a special boom. It is no more than right and proper that from such quite significant war profits a part is directed to the community. On the other hand, a much sharper evaluation is to be made in the case of that wealth which arises from intermediary trade and speculation.

8. Stamp duties and fees, even taxes that restrict the free right of disposal of elements of wealth, insofar as this disposal is not directed against the general welfare, are to be limited where possible. To this belong also the inheritance and gift taxes.

Fundamentally the tax financial policy should strive for the final goal of the "state without taxes", for it is not the task of the state to extract money from its citizens in order to perpetuate a basically false state loan economy, but to raise the general welfare of the people. The state is not there to be the interest collector for large loan capital but to protect the person and property of its state citizens and to make the natural resources of the country serviceable to the community. The means for the unproductive state tasks should, as already described, be taken primarily from the surpluses of the commercial state enterprises, and secondly from luxury taxes, thirdly from wealth and income that lie beyond that which can be obtained through the mere performance of work, and only then from the propertied middle-class, as well as from indirect taxes on semi-luxury goods whose use is not vitally necessary. And only in war-times, in which the life of the entire nation is threatened, can the state demand that even the community – as it can indeed demand military service from everybody through its service sovereignty –, and once again with special reference to the propertied classes, make its financial contribution to the conduct of the war in the form of indirect and direct taxes.

In conclusion we may say something more about the question of the "commercial state enterprises". One now prefers to point to the fact that state enterprises are not "profitable". We have already discussed at length the fundamental question of profitability.

In the effort to conduct the railways, etc. "in a business-like way", to "free them from the uneconomic state enterprise" or "to bring them into a mixed economic form" is hidden only the badly concealed desire of large loan capital to make even this considerable wealth component of the nation serviceable to itself. If the state hands over even these components of wealth, then it is fully delivered to loan capital and it has, apart from the permission to act as an interest collector for the loan capital, no more field in which it is sovereign, or in which it can operate in a regulatory manner and from which it can obtain considerable revenues for the coverage of its tasks.

The Financial Political Liberation of The State

We described first what measures are to be taken in order to make circumstances such as we experience now impossible in the future. These tasks indeed demand creative services, but they can nevertheless be achieved without the existing legal conditions having to be damaged or changed. It is different with the breaking of the existing chains of the interest-bound debt of our state to its internal and external creditors.

The measures to be taken here are in themselves extremely simple, only their execution will cause many difficulties. The remedy for the eternal interest obligation from internal loans is: the legal abolition of this interest payment. On the other hand, large loan capital will, pleading the interests of the small pensioners, raise a great hue and cry and issue the most frightful threats against a state that "tramples inviolable rights under its feet", which "commits a breach of law which will rob it of its last shred of trust". Large capital will naturally move all levers to prevent "the enormous crime against basic economic laws". Naturally! - one cannot really expect that an international

III. The State

power will suddenly renounce its claim to rulership. In this battle it is only a matter of maintaining iron nerves and not allowing oneself to be frightened by the howl of the press coolies who are maintained by high finance.

The Jew will conduct this battle with the most tenacious doggedness, for it is a matter of "his honour" as the old Rothschild said: "My money is my honour, and one who takes my money takes away my honour from me".

Now indeed their money should in no way be taken from the owners of the state bonds, but legal demands must just be removed that have in their effect become a very great injustice to the national community.

But from the viewpoint of the state, as well as from the viewpoint of the population who must raise the enormous amounts through their work in order to satisfy these "legal demands of the state creditors", it is not a matter of "legal demands" but of the greatest injustice of all times – of a lasting robbery of the working people in favour of a small section of large capitalists with state support. A state which makes the "breaking of interest slavery" a fact does not in any way commit an injustice but it atones for a quite powerful injustice for the perpetration of which it itself has performed stooge-service.

Of course this means a complete reorganisation of the present state; it must decide if it wishes to serve the whole or whether it, as now, wishes to be the bailiff of international finance. On this question there are no compromises. Here only a determined clampdown can lead to the goal and to the remedy.

The National Socialist state is indeed conscious of this powerful decision – it would be extremely difficult to take such a decisive step if we did not know exactly what we have to set up in place of the interest capitalistic economy. But because we know this, we go with the most complete certainty of victory into this greatest battle of world-history. We know that the rule of interest is built only on lies and deception and, because we know and have clearly recognised this, we know also that such a spider's web of lies and deception, however arduously it may have been spun, can be torn apart with one tug.

Only one more question, the last, must occupy us, the question: What will foreign nations say to such a radical reform and especially to a refusal of further interest payments to foreign interest creditors?

The German State on a National and Socialist Foundation

Yes, what will foreign nations say to that? This question is already in itself so extremely significant for our German distress and also for the cosmopolitan attitude of the largest circles. What in general are "foreign nations"? Are they the French, the English, the Americans? Are they the Swedes and Dutch and Norwegians? Are they the Russians or the Chinese? Or are they the Indians or the Fuegians[95] or the Congolese negroes? Indeed, all these people belong to "foreign nations" in relation to us. Now, by far the greatest number of all these "foreigners" will not say anything at all, the smallest number of Chinese, also the smallest number of Russians and French will know in general what it is about. Finally there remain the governments of our war enemies and then naturally – as the ones really interested – the Jewish international bankers, who "will say something about it". What the international finance will say to that is however very easy to answer. It will, with all the means standing at its disposal, characterise such a procedure as an unprecedented crime against cultured mankind, it will, through its own devoted press with all possible lies and distortions, raise the so-called civilised world against such an unprecedented breach of undertaken obligations, it will speak of the complete collapse of Europe, and it will attempt to incite France as the especially suited bearer of European civilisation to an open war against Germany. All that the foreign nations, that is, the Jewish high finance, will say against such an assassination attempt against the total power of the big Jewry.

One could therefore spare oneself both the question in itself and the answer. For, it is clear as daylight that that power against which the war of liberation is directed will not subject itself without a fight, since it is not a matter here of Germans, to whom the foreign interests and rights are mostly more sacred than the rights of the Germans, but of men whose most outstanding characteristic is a brutal will to power.

In all such final historical questions it is absolutely idle to make speculative observations on what the enemy will now do, for that the latter will not allow a liberation or revolt immediately is obvious. Quite different is the consideration of what means of power the opponent has at his disposal and to know what strengths one oneself disposes of. If, further, one knows precisely what one must oneself do and will do, then one must observe how the enemy will parry the attack and only then can one adopt the counter-measures. No military plan can

---

95 [The inhabitants of Tierra del Fuego, the archipelago off the southern tip of South America.]

III. The State

determine the campaign beyond the first attack, but it can indeed give the general guidelines for an energetic course of action. So also here.

In our case the opponents are hard to catch because it is a matter of an impersonal and supranational power. The campaign plan will therefore have to consider first which powers and interests do not come into consideration as opponents. This is important for not using powers unnecessarily in a direction from which no danger threatens.

Behind the question, "What will the foreign countries say to that?" hides mostly the anxiety that we will in such a case receive no credit or food or other raw materials from abroad. Now what is the situation here?

As a national economy we can in the long run pay for our imports always only through our exports, that is, exchange goods for goods, but not with paper money and not with "credits". All this works for some time, so long as the foreign countries give actual credit, that is, so long as the different foreign suppliers have faith that the German importers will pay the concerned wares with full-value money. But that is possible only if the importers have collected foreign money as exporters of German goods. The fear that we will not receive any cotton or fats, copper or fodder, on account of the refusal of international interest payments combines questions together that basically do not have anything to do with one another. Even the all-Jewish big bank power cannot in the long run prevent the surpluses in the raw material-producing countries from reaching the German factories and workplaces in some way, and likewise will the German finished goods too find their way out into the sales markets of the world. This mutual exchange of goods between the different national economies indeed takes place according to the compelling laws of supply and demand. Of course, under compulsion, and temporarily, restrictions and stoppages can occur here as we experienced it in the war, and then again in the Ruhr region.[96] But these are all forceful measures that damage the foreign countries in a similar way.

---

96 [When, in late 1922, the Germans were found to be seriously defaulting in their payment of timber and coal as war reparations to the Allies, the French and Belgians, under the direction of the French Prime Minister Raymond Poincaré, occupied the Ruhr industrial region in January 1923. The German reaction to this occupation was mostly one of passive resistance, which won the sympathy of the world and led to a "softening" of the terms of the reparations in the Dawes Pact of April 1924 (see above p.100) which also called for a withdrawal of Allied occupation troops from the Ruhr.]

The German State on a National and Socialist Foundation

We can thus suppose with certainty that wholesale trade will succeed in covering the absolutely necessary import need. There will always be neutral countries through which these imports can reach us.

Moreover, a national economy which is conscious once again of its national duties and which thereby would become again more efficient in the case of export articles can much rather count on the fact that it will regain the old trust. The temporary intermediary credits in import and export are matters of the trade houses and are based on their personal credit.

Now this question has another aspect, that is the fear of political compulsory measures on account of the suspension of the national interest payment to the war bonds and other interest-bearing bonds of the Reich or the federal states. Even this is extremely unlikely since it is a question here of the interest demands of individual private creditors of German government bonds, for whose sake hardly any political action can be taken. In fact also it has not yet occurred in the history of state bankruptcies that a military intervention followed when a state suspended its interest payment. The contrary opinion that, in this case, the French would immediately effect reprisals is in no way to be accepted on logical grounds for, otherwise, the enemies would at that time have had to intervene through military action against the decline of the German mark. The currency decline finally deprived the foreign creditors of German bonds of everything. Now our measures do not at all foresee the annulment of these internal German state debts, but only the cancellation of interest and the transformation of the bonds into bank assets. The cash payment can, on the other hand, be immediately offered to the foreign creditors.

How is it possible that in such a case, that is, when Mr. X. Illinois or Chicago receives the information from his banker that the German government is paying back the war bonds in cash and that this amount has been credited to his account, he would be very angry and set his government in motion against Germany?

A serious resistance is to be expected from no side if a nationalist German government declared the cancellation of interest from all interest-bearing bonds with a simultaneous transformation of these bonds into interest-free assets in state banks or postal cheque accounts. For us it is important that, through our measures, the community is not harmed. - the fact that resistance will be undertaken from the capitalistic side cannot constrain the liberating deed. One will see

III. The State

precisely in the case of this measure that a separation of souls will take place here and that the the closed phalanx of those who will feel in this government measure a release and liberation of work from an enormous pressure will very soon include all workers. Only the bank and stock-exchange circle and those in the circle of small pensioners trapped in their own advantages will continue to stand as their opponents.

One who works has no special interest in the fact that he receives from his temporary assets interest from the banks, much less does he have an interest in paying very high interests for credits; with his money as a working capital he wants to work and earn. For this reason all businessmen, factory owners and tradesmen will be very little interested in the maintenance of the interest capitalistic system. - This becomes clear as daylight to everybody who bears in mind that government interests - as we have shown most clearly - are only extracted through direct or indirect taxes from the work income of the productive workers.

One who has this knowledge clearly in mind cannot be swayed at any moment, for it is indeed just a fundamental principle: that the state can only give what it must once again take away from its citizens in some form.

The interests for the interest payment of the state must in all circumstances be drawn from the productive workers. No worker is excluded from this principle, least of all the manual labourer who has no interest-bearing bonds at his disposal. This situation hits him hardest, for the direct and especially the indirect taxes also affect him most severely. Now, that precisely the worker is called on for the tax through the direct income tax in the form of income deduction before all other circles has already made the worker clairvoyant regarding these matters; the same is true also of all wage- and salary-earners. To be sure, these circles are much less conscious of the much more radical indirect taxes - although they feel them mostly in inflation, as was described in the chapter on "Inflation". Indirect tax is the most unsocial tax. It burdens work in favour of pure loan capital. Nobody can withdraw from it, and therefore it oppresses the one who has the least income most severely. On the other hand, the indirect taxes - the coal-, salt-, match-, sugar-, beer- and drink taxes, the personal transport taxes, etc. - do not disturb in the least the owner of large capital wealth.

The German State on a National and Socialist Foundation

One therefore from the circle of workers who is an opponent of such a liberating deed can be that only through lack of knowledge and understanding of these connections.

The last and hardest thing that we should still deal with in this chapter is the question of the removal of the international interest obligations – in other words, the refusal of further interest payments for the war debts.

This question is most closely bound with the German historical question, indeed it is actually the German question in general, for it says: Does the German nation want freedom or slavery?

We know that, in such final questions, only the determined will can determine and achieve victory – the reply to this question therefore goes far beyond the range of financial political observations. But it is essential that a nation that must strive for its freedom know that its slavery is in the very first place a financial political one, that here politics and economics are most closely related. But precisely this is the new thing about the present situation that it is ruled by financial power political viewpoints and that the military power political viewpoints come only in second place.

We can indeed speak of the Mammonistic age as of a new epoch. The god Mammon has ascended the throne of this world. Emperor and king bow before him. The parliaments and governments are his submissive servants. He has been able to yoke large movements – like the striving of the wage-earners for their improvement. International capital has likewise made the presses of the world serviceable to its goals – as it has also made itself the administrator of the cultural wealth and the adulterator of every national indigenous art and literature.

As the most outstanding bearers of this Mammonistic infestation and rule of the world we have recognised the Jews and so the circle of our knowledge is closed once again with the question of all questions – the Jewish question.

The solution of the interest problem is the solution of the Jewish question. The solution of the interest problem in the sense of our explanations is the breaking of the Jewish world-rule, because it smashes the power of world Jewry – its financial power.

III. The State

But the solution of the interest problem is, moreover, in a constructive sense, at the same time also the solution of the social question.

A refusal of every interest and duty payments to the war debts would place international finance, or France, before the question of its takeover of the the entire financial administration of all of Germany. If all the taxes of the Reich are removed that now serve the interest payment to the enemy, this would mean first of all internally a redemption from the crazy tax oppression, a great social political deed of the greatest scope, and the enemy would have to try to develop its own financial administration in Germany.

But if the German people saw the French or Jewish tax collector sitting in every tax- and pension office, and if the best cows were taken from the stalls of the farmers by these foreign oppressors – then the anger and indignation would perhaps become soon so strong that one night would sweep the foreign spectre away with a bloody broom and free Germany.

Whether, in general, a military power would take on such an enterprise in the service of the financial power is therefore still very questionable.

The prospects of our will to liberation are in no way so unfavourable as they may have seemed at first – on the contrary. The very first time that Germany unanimously refused the handing over of its "war heroes", with this "no" the spectre was finished.

Now international finance will certainly seek other methods, especially the method of the boycott and the entire strangulation of the international market. That it will not succeed in the latter may likewise be certain, and also the boycott of German goods would direct Germany, at first just in its economic activity, and for a time also exclusively, to its internal market. It would therefore be here also only the task of a skilled domestic policy - specially through generous promotion in the field of housing construction - to overcome the critical times and to use them for the welfare of the people, until the new paths to the world are determined.

This opening up of new paths to the world will occur through the breaking of the Jewish domination even among other nations, for the way of the individual nations too to a healthy national economy can only be through their being cured of their domestic poisoning by the Jewish-Mammonistic poison. Then the natural paths of a healthy

The German State on a National and Socialist Foundation

international trade and economic commerce between the nations will open up by themselves – and mankind, freed of the Jewish oppression, will experience an age of unprecedented prosperity – and, above all, *Germany - the heart of the world.*

www.ingramcontent.com/pod-product-compliance
Lightning Source LLC
Chambersburg PA
CBHW052101230426
43662CB00036B/1721